ASPECTS OF THE THEOLOGY OF KARL BARTH

William P. Anderson

UNIVERSITY
PRESS OF
AMERICA

Library of Congress Catalog Card Number: **81-40163**

To Carolyn --

    With love and affection

        always!

ACKNOWLEDGMENTS

With sincere appreciation, the author acknowled
ges the use of the following works by permission:

Church Dogmatics, Volumes I - IV
by Karl Barth
Published by T & T Clark
Used by permission.

The Epistle to the Romans
by Karl Barth
Published by Oxford University Press
Used by permission.

The Word of God and The Word of Man
by Karl Barth
Published by Harper and Row
Used by permission.

The Humanity of God
by Karl Barth
Copyright C. D. Deans 1960
Used by permission

Dogmatics in Outline
by Karl Barth
Published by Philosophical Library, Inc.
Used by permission.

Revolutionary Theology in the Making, Barth-Thur-
neysen Correspondence, 1914-1925, Translated by
James D. Smart
Copyright M. E. Bratcher 1964
Published by John Knox Press
Used by permission.

God Was In Christ
by Donald Baillie
Published by Charles Scribner's Sons
Used by permission.

The Triumph of Grace in the Theology of Karl Barth
by G. C. Berkouwer
Published by William B. Eerdmans Publishing Company
Used by permission.

TABLE OF CONTENTS

PREFACE

This work is the product of many years of study and reflection. Parts of it were originally developed in competition for the Fellowship in Systematic Theology at Princeton Theological Seminary; other parts were the outgrowth of this Fellowship and the continued fascination with this great Swiss theologian, a fascination which eventually took me to the land of his birth and the place of his teaching. However, one of the most memorable experiences of my life was the great joy and privilege that was mine as I listened to Karl Barth lecture, debate, and dialogue with faculty, students and friends during his visit to the United States in 1962 for the Sesquicentennial Celebration of the Theological Seminary at Princeton. Although I have never become a "Barthian" and indeed he, perhaps, was not a Barthian himself, I have never ceased to be captivated by his challenge to the Church and the World.

Karl Barth, during his lifetime and since his death, has been adored and scorned; he has been called a "Jesu-ologist," a "Christomonist," and a "Modernist," among other things. However, whatever he may be called, he most certainly almost singlehandedly reversed the tide of Protestant theology in the early part of this century, spoke out forcefully and prophetically against the rising demon in the Third Reich in the 1930's, being one of the chief authors of the <u>Theological Declaration of Barmen</u> in 1934, and until his death in 1968 was perhaps the leading Protestant theologian in the world (although I suspect some would like to argue that point). Christ is certainly, in all of this, first and foremost in the mind and thought of Karl Barth, for Barth was a devoted Christian.

This present work is a modest attempt to present some of his basic concepts, e.g., Revelation, the doctrine of the Trinity, the development of his Christology from its early stages to its mature presentation in the Fourth Volume of the

xi

Dogmatics, and to do this in a critical fashion.
Much has been cited from the works of Barth himself
in order that the reader may experience the genius
of Barth himself. Hopefully, some will learn to
love and appreciate the scholar and the man
through these efforts.

In all these years of reflection and pre-
paration, I have been indebted to many people ---
too many to recall, but I am chiefly indebted to
my family, who often find it difficult to live
with, and to put up with, the procrastinations and
idiosyncracies of a theologian. And so I express
my deepest and most sincere appreciation to my
daughter, Janice, who in many ways is conceptually
a carbon copy of her father, and to my sons Bill
and Kevin who, in their own ways, chide and challenge
their father. Without any of them life would not
be the same. In the end, however, I owe my deepest
gratitude to my faithful wife, Carolyn, for her
love, her support which is always in evidence,
and her tireless efforts in my behalf. To her I
dedicate this my first published work.

William P. Anderson
Dayton, Ohio
May, 1981

CHAPTER I

AN EXAMINATION OF THE DEVELOPMENT

OF THE

EARLY THEOLOGY OF KARL BARTH

Beginning to study the theology of Karl Barth
is tantamount to trying to read all of the books
in any substantial library, and to keep pace with
all new publications; one simply cannot keep
pace with the task. So here also we find ourselves facing a monumental task. Be that as it
may, let us delineate here the form that this
discussion will take, or perhaps more correctly,
this analysis will take. We shall consider, and
in the following sequence, these particular areas:
a consideration of the historical situation
surrounding Karl Barth, including some aspects of
his early schooling, which played a very important
role in his theological development. Furthermore,
in this period, Barth was influenced by certain
individuals, both contemporary and significant
figures from the past. We shall, therefore,
briefly discuss, Franz Overbeck, the Blumhardts,
and Soren Kierkegaard. We shall then endeavor to
see how these influences (certainly not exhaustive),
historical and personal, manifested themselves in
the cataclysmic period of Karl Barth represented
in his Epistle to the Romans. We shall conclude by
sketching, perhaps all too briefly, primarily
through his own remarks, Barth's consideration of
his development up to the time of his death in 1968.

In his early period, it may be said that the
theology of Karl Barth falls into the thought-
patterns and form of what is commonly referred to
as Neo-Protestantism. By this we generally mean
that he was of the theological tradition of religious individualism, represented above all by the
great German theologian Friedrich Schleiermacher
and formulated under the impact of, and influence
of, Romantic Idealistic philosophy. Barth describes this early theology as "a theology in the
succession of Descartes, primarily and definitely
interested in human, and particularly, the Christian
religion within the framework of our modern outlook on the world, considering God, His work, and
His Word from this point of view, and adopting the
critical attitude toward the message of the Bible
and esslesiastical tradition -- to this extent,
and anthropological theology."[1]

This was the type of theological, philosophical, and Biblical training and tradition that Karl Barth took with him into the parish, a factor of substantial significance, as we shall see shortly. He was to discover that the startling characteristic elements of the New Testament message were being neutralized, and domesticated, in the world and its culture.

It is no secret that Barth had an inquiring mind, indeed a relentlessly inquiring mind, which had always insisted upon reflection, serious reflection, upon the questionableness of the entire theological process.[2] In this process two or three factors are of significance when related to his particular situation. One of these factors was his pastorate in Geneva and Safenwil and his discovery of the "strange new world of the scriptures,"[3] as he labored in his duties. It was here that Barth encountered difficulties; it was here that he saw, as a preacher and as a theologian, that something was missing. At Geneva, where he was vicar to the German speaking congregation, Barth preached in the same lecture hall in which John Calvin labored and very carefully Barth worked his way through the Institutes. He reexamined, at this time, the work of Schleiermacher but generally considered himself in the Ritschlian tradition, shaped by Wilhelm Hermann. Nevertheless, Barth was uneasy about his theological pursuits. As he himself indicates:

> To the prevailing tendency of about 1910 among the younter followers of Albrecht Ritschl I attached myself with passable conviction. Yet it was not without a certain alienation in view of the issue of this school in the philosophy of Ernst Troeltsch, in which I found myself disappointed in regard to what interested me in theology, although for the time being I did not see a better way before me.[4]

This difficulty, which may be characterized by

uneasiness of hunger, was brought home with full force upon Barth. Again, as he himself puts it:

> I myself know what it means year in year
> out to mount the steps of the pulpit,
> conscious of the responsibility to under-
> stand and interpret, and longing to fulfill
> it; and yet, utterly incapable, because at
> the University I had never been brought
> beyond that well-know "Awe in the presence
> of History" which in the end means no more
> than that all hope of engaging in the dig-
> nity of understanding and interpretation
> has been surrendered....It was this miser-
> able situation that compelled me as a
> pastor to undertake a more precise under-
> standing and interpretation of the Bible.[5]

In this context Barth takes exception with exegetes such as Adolf Julicher, whom he calls typical, for dismissing various aspects of the Epistle to the Romans as peculiar religious thoughts, experiences, etc., of the Apostle Paul, whenever a difficult passage was encountered. So, Barth thrust himself into the struggle within the pages of the New Testament. Barth was determined to hear the Word of God, as it came from God Himself, as it came from above, not as it came from within man, diluted by some humanistic, culturistic phenomenon. This also is testified to by his later writing, The Humanity of God, where he recalls, "Evangelical theology almost all along the line, certainly in all its representative forms, and tendencies, had become 'religionistic,' 'anthropocentric,' and in this sense 'humanistic'."[6] This is very similar to his statement in the commentary on the Romans. In effect, what did the prevailing theology know and say of the deity of God? It said precious little and when it did, it spoke of God, but in reality it was speaking in a veiled fashion about man. Perhaps, if we may be permitted to put it in the form of a cliche: "to speak about God is to speak about man in a loud voice;" or, "man was made great at the expense of

God." God was being reduced to nothing more than
a pious notion, a mystical, pietistic expression
or a symbolic oscillation between the inner heights
and depths of man's inner being.[7] To Barth the
theology of that day was acting, _eritis_ _sicut_ _Deus_;
it was erecting its own "Tower of Babel," endeavor-
ing to change the righteousness of God into human
righteousness,[8] right down to, and including, most
especially, religious righteousness. To this end,
to these activities Barth directs himself with
devastating power, causing great turmoil in the
ranks of his fellow scholars. Not only is this
evident in the early essay referred to above
(note 7), but more especially in the Romans where
we read such statements as "The frontier of religion is the line of death which separates flesh
from spirit, time from eternity, the human possibility from the possibility of God."[9] And further,
"we...are compelled to recognize, whether we
acknowledge it or not, that our own concrete status
in the world of time and of men and of things lies
under the shadow of death."[10] Or, as he wrote
concerning Chapter V, verse 20 of Paul's letter
to the Romans, "Is not the dialectical balance
between sin and righteousness replaced in religion
by a healthy, vigorous, divine humanity and a
human divinity?...Yes! the relation with God has
its human, historical subjective side."[11] But
Barth is quick to point out, with great emphasis,
that this activity is a divine possibility and
cannot as such be transformed into a human endeavor.
Again, as Karl Barth puts it:

> This religion which we are able to detect
> in ourselves and others is that of human
> possibility, and as such, it is a most
> precarious attempt to imitate the flight
> of a bird. And so, if religion be under-
> stood as a concrete, comprehensible, and
> historical phenomenon in the world of men
> and of sin and death --- it must be aban-
> doned....the boldest speculations of
> religion...end, that is to say, in the
> territory of the "No-God,' of this world,
> where they can be honored as 'Life' and

as the 'Kingdom of God,' as 'reality' and
as 'the otherworldliness.' --- No more can
be said POSITIVELY about religion than that
its purest, and noblest and most tenacious
achievements mankind reaches, and indeed
must reach, its highest pinnacle of human
possibility. But even so religion remains
a human achievement.[12]

From these few statements we may discern that
Barth was determined to hear the Word of God itself,
that he was attempting to plunge theology into a
new direction with a devastating attack upon the
prevailing thought. With this message Karl Barth's
commentary on the Romans landed like a bombshell in
the playground of the theologians (as Karl Adam
once put it). Looking back at this, and assessing
its impact, Barth made the following observation:

> As I look back upon my course, I seem to
> myself as one who, ascending the dark
> staircase of a church tower and trying to
> steady himself, reached for the bannister,
> but got hold of the bell rope instead. To
> his horror, he had then to listen to what
> the great bell had sounded over him and
> not over him alone.[13]

That this is true can easily be seen by the many
private debates that occur in the pleroma of pre-
faces to the various editions of this commentary
on the Romans, i.e., discussions of criticisms by
Jülicher, Wernle, Lietzmann and Harnack, and the
historians in general; discussions surrounding
such charges as, "the enemy of historical criticism,"
"esotericism," "Marcionism," and "Biblicism," to
cite just a few.

It was not, however, only the academic, the
theological and the philosophical presuppositions
that brought their forces to bear on Barth at this
time. It was also the manner in which these various
disciplines manifested themselves in their particular
adherents. Two events, in particular, were quite
significant. In 1914, Ernst Troeltsch, a recog-

nized leader, a systematic theologian of the modern
theology, crossed over from the theological faculty
to the faculty of philosophy. In addition to this
event there was also that momentous day, also in
1914, August to be more exact, about which Barth
himself writes:

> For me personally one day at the beginning
> of August that year stampted itself as
> dies ater. It was that on which 93 German
> intellectuals came out with a manifesto
> supporting the war policy of Kaiser William
> II and his counsellors, and among them I
> found to my horror the names of nearly all
> my theological teachers whom up to then I
> had religiously honored. Disillusioned
> by their conduct, I perceived that I should
> not be able any longer to accept their
> ethics and dogmatics, their Biblical
> exegesis, their interpretation of history,
> that at least for me the theology of the
> nineteenth century had no future.[14]

These events had tremendous consequences in the life
and work of Karl Barth and as we have indicated the
immediate turn took its form in the search for new
foundations. As Barth says in his essay, The Humanity of God, "The change of direction had a pronounced
critical and polemical character. It came to completion gradually when viewed in terms of time, but
a sudden conversion when viewed in terms of events."[15]

Thus the eyes of Barth were opened, as it were,
opened to the fact that God just might want to be
God and to speak quite differently than being entombed
in a musty shrine of Christian self-righteousness.
It is, then, without a doubt that it was the failure
to see God clearly in his theological upbringing,
the failure of Neo-Protestantism in the human situation in which he found himself, the inadequacy he
felt as a preacher of the Word that helped to lead
this theologian, even if we may not always be in
agreement with him, to this theological revolution.
Barth saw a facuum and wanted to fill the gap in
preaching with solid exegesis and theology, which

for him could only be found in a fundamental dialogue with God Himself. In an address to a group
of ministers in July of 1922, meeting in Schulp-
forta, Karl Barth himself summarizes the context
within which his theological re-orientation took
place:

> For twelve years I was a minister, as all
> of you are, I had my theology. It was not
> really mind, to be sure, but that of my
> unforgotten teacher Wilhelm Hermann,
> grafted upon the principles which I had
> learned, less consciously than unconsciously,
> in my native home---the principles of those
> Reformed Churches which today I represent
> and am honored to represent in an official
> capacity. Once in the ministry, I found
> myself growing away from these theological
> habits of thought and being forced back
> at every point more and more to the minis-
> ter's problem, the sermon. I sought to find
> my way between the problem of human life
> on the one hand and the content of the
> Bible on the other. As a minister I wanted
> to speak to the people in the infinite con-
> tradiction of their life, but to speak the
> no less infinite message of the Bible, which
> was as much of a riddle as life.[16]

These were some of the historical and early influences that led Karl Barth to his epoch-making revolt.

    Other individuals influenced Barth during this
period as well, and did so in, what we may call,
a more positive way. At least their influence
created or helped to create the "new starting point"
in Karl Barth's theology. Some of the men with
whom Barth had an affinity were: Issac A. Dorner,
the Blumhardts -- father and son -- Soren Kierkegaard, Hermann Friedrich Kohlbrugge, Herman Kutter,
Julius Muller, Franz Overbeck and A.F.C. Vilmar.
In a variety of ways these men stood over against
the dominant stream of nineteenth century theology,
i.e., the theological line running from Friedrich
Schleiermacher through Albrecht Ritschl to Wilhelm

Hermann and Ernst Troeltsch. By way of illustration we shall briefly consider the influence of
Franz Overbeck, the Blumhardts, and, of course,
that of Soren Kierkegaard.

A. FRANZ OVERBECK

Franz Overbeck was Professor of Critical
Theology at the University of Basel from
1872-1897.[17] It was within the historical
situation which we have been describing, and
with an insatiable desire to really render unto
God the Glory, Majesty and Praise due Him, glory
and power that had been vastly ignored by the
prevalent theologies, it was with this background that Barth read and appreciated Franz
Overbeck and saw in him the positive intention
behind his attack upon historical Christianity.
He criticized what Barth himself was not criti-
cizing. That is to say, Overbeck rendered a
severe and trenchant criticism of historical
Christianity which he contrasted with the original historic foundation of the Church in Christ
and the Apostles. Historical Christianity was
seen as a development down through the centuries
and, as such, was subordinated to time, to the
time of the world, whereas originally, (Urgeschichte)
in its own history before "historical Christianity"
arose, Christianity was the product of the supernatural Kingdom of God which binds and makes
relative all things of the world and history.[18]
Furthermore, by Urgeschichte he meant the events
for which the Biblical witnesses were a divine
history taking place in the midst of history then
and there, e.g., in the words of the creed,
"under Pontius Pilate," a history in which all
history has its mysterious center because in it
the eternal decisions are made which determine
the life of all men at all times. The modern
theologians were seen as perpetuating and advoca-
ting this historical Christianity and as betraying
Christianity itself. It was call the "religion
of Satan;" it was also described as a "worldly-
wise religion" that very conveniently puts God
into a bag.[19]

Overbeck, then, had attacked the Christian
character of the theology of his century long
before Karl Barth especially with reference to
Adolf von Harnack's historical representation of
early Christianity. The impetus for this was the
posthumously edited throughts and observations
published in 1919 under the title Christentum
und Kultur. The real seriousness with which Barth
took the strictures of the Basel historian, who
stood on the boundary between skepticism and
inspired criticism, can be seen in a study
produced under the title On the Inner Situation
of Christianity. It seems clear that Overbeck
enabled Barth to perceive the theological task
more clearly even though the study caused much
head-shaking and much opposition. Karl Barth
seems to take great delight in expressing the
support of Franz Overbeck's widow as to the
correctness of his interpretation of her husband's
views. Thus Barth writes to his good friend and
colleague Eduard Thurneysen:

> ...Another afternoon I paid a visit to
> Frau Professor Overbeck. She is fully
> abreast of affairs, a lively, sensible old
> lady, who received me very warmly and
> portrayed her husband for me in a way that
> simply tallies to the hairbreath with our
> conception of him. It will be all right for
> our booklet (On the Inner Situation of
> Christianity) to appear since everything
> is in order. And "we" shall laugh at the
> Basel - know-it-alls more than they at
> us.20

It goes without saying, from the circumstances
as we have described them, that neither Overbeck
nor Barth's evaluation and appreciation of Overbeck's
intentions were received with not a little opposition. However, their critics failed to see beyond
the devastating criticism to the real breakthrough,
the real desire for emancipation from the chains
of historical Christendom and its worldly perversion
of the Church. This renewal, or this emancipation,
could only be achieved at the cost of "historical

Christianity," only at the cost of what we have all
traditionally called religion. This was the question that Barth had to evaluate and which he did
so graphically in the Epistle to the Romans (especially pp. 229-270).

Two important points emerge out of Karl
Barth's appreciation of Franz Overbeck. First:
he sees clearly the need for a radical change
in his presuppositions if theology is to forge
ahead; he sees that Overbeck's dangerous, but
necessary, criticism of historical Christianity
must be taken seriously, that there must be a
hiatus between the gospel and its worldly perversion, between Christianity and culture. However, these criticisms must also be openings for
new paths of a positive message. Second:
we may legitimately say that the experience of
being exposed to Overbeck together with the setting
in which Barth found himself provided the material
substance, or at least greatly contributed to it,
for the very famous NO portion of his dialectic;
indeed here we see the formulation of a significant part of what became known as Barth's
KRISIS THEOLOGY. It is a narrow door, but it can,
and it did, open the way for a positive message
in the case of Karl Barth.

B. JOHANN CHRISTOPH BLUMHARDT
AND
CHRISTOPH BLUMHARDT

Another powerful influence in the development
of Barth's theology, at this stage, was Johann
Christoph Blumhardt and his son Christoph with
their distinctive emphasis upon the eschatological;
the fresh understanding of the Kingdom of God
as the breaking into the world of God's unutterable
compassion in victorious Grace which was both
the judgment of the world and the great supernatural saving event of the gospel. Here is the
pouring out of God Himself in love upon the world
in Jesus Christ so that all agony and hurt is taken
upon Himself, and so that the purpose of His love
will be victorious, come what may. Undoubtedly,
this is hidden from our eyes and is only visible

to the eye of faith. Nevertheless, the day will
come when the work of Deus absconditus will come
to an end and the victory of Christ and His Kingdom will be clearly manifest. Johann Christoph
Blumhardt characterized this theme by the phrase
"Jesus is Victor!" In Jesus Christ the victory
over the powers of darkness was forever secured
and the whole world is now claimed for His Kingdom.

But this eschatological intervention has
already occurred. Christoph Blumhardt, who at
one time pointed to the pressing need for the proclamation of the Kingdom of God and the burning
hope for its consummation in a coming day of God
when the whole earth is filled with the gloria
Dei, also states:

> Just don't think that it is all in the
> "hereafter." That's a big lie; you can
> wait a long time for that. Nothing will
> be revealed in the hereafter that is not
> already found here. The earth is the
> goal of God. It is here that the inheri-
> tance is to be received, it comes with
> the creation, not with philosophy or
> theology.[21]

Thus "Jesus is Victor" and "Man is God's" were
themes important to, and advocated, presented and
lived by the Elder and Younger Blumhardts.

Because this supernatural Kingdom breaks
in upon the world now, the theologians, the preachers
and indeed all Christians have the task of relating
it to the whole realm of human life. Every facet of
life is deeply involved in this eschatological
message, every facet of life is filled with a
new sense of urgency. The eschatological has
entered the present; it is, as it were, shaping
it, for here we see in Jesus Christ, Divine compassion for humanity. (We should point out,
however, that Barth broke with the radical movement
of the Younger Blumhardt et.al., when they combined
the Christian expectation with the socialist
expectation of the future.) Thus we may see here,
as we have said negatively of Franz Overbeck, the

-13-

positive: the YES of God's grace, the other side
of the dialectic, passing through the narrow doors
of negation.   This means that theology must face
the Last Things (which it had not been doing in
the opinion of Barth), it must come up against
the realities of the Ultimate, it must come up
against the judgment of God and yet proceed forward
under their impact. Here we may see the significance of the resurrection. "It is sown in
corruption; it is raised in incorruption; it is
sown in dishonor; it is raised in glory; it is
sown in weakness; it is raised in power."[22]

C. SÖREN KIERKEGAARD

Theologically and philosophically it is undoubtedly Sören Kierkegaard who had the greatest
impact upon Karl Barth, at least in the early
stages of his revolutionary thought. That seems
to be obviously apparent in the indebtedness of
his thinking to Kierkegaard's attack upon all
direct communication and easy living, i.e., living
comfortably with God.

> May we be preserved from the blasphemy of
> men who without being terrified and afraid
> in the presence of God, without the agony
> of death which is the birthpang of faith,
> without the trembling which is the first
> requirement of adoration, without the panic
> of the possibility of scandal, hope to have
> direct knowledge of that which cannot be
> directly known...and do not rather say that
> He was truly and verily God because He was
> beyond our comprehension.[23]

We should also point out that, if we take it
at its plain face value, and I do not see any reason
at this point why we should not, Barth states that
he is indebted to Kierkegaard for his "system"
(in Romans) insofar as it can be said that he had
one.

> If I have a system, it is limited to a
> recognition of what Kierkegaard has called

-14-

the "infinite qualitative distinction"
between time and eternity, and to my regarding
this as possessing negative as well as positive significance. God is in heaven and
thou art on earth. The relation between such
a God and such a man, is for me the central
theme of the Bible and the essence of Philosophy.[24]

Barth apparently was interested in the Danish
philosopher-theologian's emphasis upon that explosive
force of the invasion of God in His Godness into time
and human existence, which was expressed by paradox
and dialectic. For example: the emphasis upon the
infinite qualitative distinction between Time and
Eternity was not based, as we might expect, upon
some abstract and distant deity, but rather upon the
nearness, the closeness, the impact of God in all
His majesty and Godness upon man. Indeed this is
the great significance of Jesus Christ that Barth,
following Soren Kierkegaard, was trying to recover
and restore. Furthermore, Barth's frequent references to "paradox," "decision," and "krisis" in the
attempt to describe the divine-human encounter are
all reminiscent of Soren Kierkegaard.

The use of this dialectical method so prominent
in the Commentary on the Romans is what gave rise to
the designation of Barth's theology as "dialectical"
or "krisis" theology. It was the adoption of this
Kierkegaardian principle which aids us in account-
ing for this characterization of his thought. Thus
in contrast to his earlier thought --- typical of
19th Century Liberalism --- where we find a greater
stress on the continuity between man and God,
earth and heaven, immanence and trancendence, at
this point Barth was in need of some method by which
he could point to the "infinite qualitative distinction" between God and man, between time and eternity.

There were several factors which commended the
dialectical method. First: as Barth himself put it
in an address delivered to Freunde der Christlichen
Welt (Friends of the Christian World) in October of
1922, "there is an unwavering insight into the fact

that the living truth, the determining content of
any real utterance concerning God, is that God
(but really God!) becomes man (but really man!)"[25]
Second: dialectics recognizes that all theology
is a dialogue between God and man. There must be
speech and response here, question and answer, yes
and no. Further, in order for there to be any
real understanding, this dialogue must be continuous. Thus this answer again becomes the question.
The movement involves two key figures: God and man.
And the ultimate source of all dialectical thinking for Barth is the God-man, Jesus Christ. As
this name involves both God and man, we are prohibited, if we are dialecticians, to regard this
as one word. From this center all thought proceeds
dialectically. Certainly man will search for the
one word which will overcome the paradoxes inherent
in this method. However, whenever this occurs,
man is guilty of overlooking the fact that all
theologizing is fragmentary in nature. All theology
must be, therefore, theologia viatorum (pilgrim
theology) for no human word can give expression
to the divine truth in its entirety or purity.
This belongs to God alone --- who is Himself the
truth. As Barth states in the Christliche Dogmatik:

> He [God] speaks the one undialectical word.
> He utters the Amen which settles matters ---
> which does not stand in need of further sup-
> plementation. He dissolves the disturbing
> "and". His theology, his knowledge and speak-
> ing about Himself is no theologia viatorum.
> It is the simplest and most decisive reason
> for the exclusive possibility of dialectical
> theology. It must, however, be true that the
> proper, the final, the decisive word be left
> to God.[26]

This position taken by Barth led some of his critics
to misunderstand his primary point. As John Godsey
indicates to us, "Barth's critics were quick to
point out that, according to his Christian Dogmatics,
there seemed to be two bases for significant assertions about the Word of God, the revelation of God
in Jesus Christ and the hearing man; as well as

two methodologies, the phenomenological and the
existential. Barth realized to his horror that
he had not succeeded in avoiding at least the
appearance of grounding theology in anthropology, which was precisely what he wanted to avoid."[27]
His critics perceived him to be a philosophical
dialectician. However, Barth's main concern was
theological. He adopted the dialectical method
as the medium by which he could point to the
message of the Word of God to man as he stands
in the situation of "krisis," as he stands between
time and eternity. This was, for Karl Barth, a
sign of God's judgment upon all human attempts to
control, manipulate and domesticate God and His
revelation. Most especially, Barth was determined
to show that the "NO" of God's judgment fell upon
man's piety, religion, philosophy and morality
because all of these attempts by man, represented
man's attempts at self-redemption. As Paul Tillich
advises us:

> Barth's Commentary on the Romans...was
> neither a commentary nor a system, but
> a prophetic call addressed to religion and
> culture, to acknowledge the divinity of
> the divine and to dissolve the Neo-Protes-
> tant synthesis between God's and man's
> creativity.[28]

Ultimately because of the possibility of misunderstanding and misrepresentation Barth concluded
that a new start had to be made. Indeed just as
he once had to re-write Der Römerbrief, he determined that it was necessary to rewrite his prolegomena to Dogmatics. Leaving existentialism behind,
he turned to Church Dogmatics based on the
analogy of faith, emphasizing the act of God in
His revelation, grounded in God's Word to men ---
Jesus Christ.

One may see the cooperative influences of
Overbeck, the Blumhardts and Kierkegaard in ferment.
However, whereas Overbeck saw the death of historical Christianity when measured by the absolute
standards of God and the gospel, when confronted

with the KRISIS, Barth, on the other hand, saw the
whole of humanity confronted and dissolved; he saw
the whole world threatened.

The Word of God is the transformation of
everything that we know as Humanity,
Nature and History and must therefore
be apprehended as the negation of the
starting-point of every system which we
are capable of conceiving. The mission
of the Son is the divine answer to the
last insoluble question which is forced
upon the man of this world as a consequence
of the dominion of sin. It cannot
therefore be identified with any human
answer, not even with any of those
answers which men disguise as penultimate
and soluble questions. The divine answer
is given only in the veritably final and
veritably human answer. The divine answer
is the righteousness of God, of God alone.[29]

This was a dangerous challenge, this point where the
thoughts of these men seem to converge, for it demanded
a theology that would face these problems, that would
set itself against time, that was prepared for the
absurd, the presence of God in space and time,
and therefore the apocalyptic relevance of Jesus
in our existence.

Barth very correctly maintains that these were
influences upon him, but equally manifests the
position that it was the stone-wall of God's deity
as the theme of the Bible that enabled him as a
theologian, and as a preacher, and as a minister,
to understand the voice of the Old and New Testaments.[30]
However, we should add, that he found a ready ally
in the Dane, Kierkegaard, was also quite true. For
it was Kierkegaard's concept of God as Subject, not
Subjectivity, that Barth came to realize; the
truth of the Incarnation encounters us objectively,
which calls into question any illusion etc., that
truth arises from within man himself. Barth relates
this to the sovereignty of God, to the Lordship of
Christ and also to the commandment of love to our
fellowmen, carefully guarding against the possibility

-18-

of any religious individualism of a pietistic
nature. So we see that God is both Subject and
Object and that this is always the starting-point
of theology.[31] This perspective helped Barth to
see clearly that pietism, modern theology,
liberalism, had read the New Testament backwards
and had failed to see that:

> Christ is the absolutely new from above;
> the way, the truth and the life of God
> among men; the Son of Man in Whom humanity
> becomes aware of its immediacy to God.
> But keep your distance! No mental appre-
> hension of the form of this truth, however
> subtle that apprehension may be, can re-
> place or obscure the true transcendence
> of its content.[32]

Neo-Protestantism had been reading things backwards
far too long; it was reversing the gospel of election
and grace and traveling a private road to God, and
purely under its own power. Barth, in turn, endea-
vored to set things straight, at least as he perceived them, in order that the gospel might be
heard as the gospel.

We have now seen some evidence of the historical situation in which Barth was placed and some
of the various influences of a personal nature
that helped to shape his new theological outlook
and perspective. At this juncture, we see him
with a strong dialectical emphasis, which is
only a natural consequence of what we have already
indicated. For if Barth in his first phase was,
in some measure, within the patterns of Neo-Protestantism, then his second phase was necessarily
one which sought to break loose from these patterns,
and turn against that mainstream of theology. This
is especially evident in his second edition of the
commentary on the Epistle to the Romans.

These new thoughts and patterns became known
as, "the theology of KRISIS," "Dialectical theology,"
"the wholly-otherness of God," and as diastasis, or
the distance, the separation between God's way and
man's ways, God's thoughts and man's thoughts,

between the gospel and humanism, between the Word of God and the word of man. Barth found deep dissatisfaction with the great subjectivism of Protestant theology, which, in effect, replaced God with man.

Thinking of ourselves what can be thought only of God, we are unable to think of Him more highly than we think of ourselves. Being to ourselves what God ought to be to us, He is no more to us than we are to ourselves. This secret identification of ourselves with God carries with it our isolation from Him. The little god must, quite appropriately, dispossess the great God. Men have <u>imprisoned</u> and encased the <u>truth</u> --- the righteousness of God; they have trimmed it to their own measure, and thereby robbed it both of its earnestness and of its significance. They have made it ordinary, harmless and useless; and thereby transformed it into untruth.[33]

Despite the great thundering <u>Krisis</u>, despite the great judgment, the infinite qualitative distinction between God and man, time and eternity etc., there can be no doubt that the great positive theme of the commentary and his related works of the period under consideration, including his sermons, is the <u>saving grace</u> and <u>compassion of God</u>, grace that is both the forgiveness of God and the self-consciousness of the new man. It is an answer to man's deepest questions concerning human existence. As Professor G. C. Berkouwer suggests, this is no desparation-theology, but rather this <u>Krisis</u> and this <u>diastasis</u> can only be understood as a divine <u>YES</u> resounding in and through judgment and separation. Here the realization of God as God and man as man takes place.[34] But this is not our doing:

We are not in a position to say anything which is relevant concerning grace and sin, until our perception has been sharpened and we are protected from pantheism

-20-

by being reminded of the critical significance of the death of Christ; until we
have been liberated from obsession with
the problem concerning what we can do or
not do. Grace is the Kingdom of God, His
rule and power and dominion. Grace is
readily contrasted with the whole realm
of human possibility, the sphere of the
sovereignty of sin. Through grace, on
account of this contrast, lies beyond
all human possibility, yet nevertheless,
for the same reason, it judges human life
and launches a disturbing attack upon it.
Insofar as in this contrast God is encountered, human life is refashioned
and provided with a new hope and a new
promise.35

We have spoken sufficiently, at least for the
scope of this analysis, of the historical and
personal influences on Karl Barth's early theology.
At this time, let us briefly see how the insights
he gained from these experiences manifested themselves as he considered such problems as (1) sin,
(2) eschatology and (3) dialectical thought.

D. THE EARLY BARTH

(1)

Barth began, as we have noted, in the tradition
of Immanuel Kant and Friedrich Schleiermacher. That
is: sin, the problem of ethics and the problem of
evil were seen and expressed in the peculiar greatness and dignity of man. These expressions, of
course, were in need of explanation and they were
explained --- naturally. But to these problems
Barth addressed himself by insisting that these
questions must be answered sub specie aeternitatis,
in the terms of Martin Luther, coram Deo.

Barth faced the problem of ethics by locking
at it from the ultimate perspective of eternity.
This does not cut it off at proximity, but rather
goes beyond to the standard which is not part of our

-21-

existence.[36] Looked at from the right perspective,
Neo-Protestantism, on this point, collapsed on
every front. It seemed to possess the feeling
that man could go onward and upward forever, and
under his own power, dignity and honor. In other
words, the only answer for our questions is not
man but God Himself and God's conduct toward us;
that is to say, in His grace and the way in which
His grace justifies the ungodly. Through our
doom we are able to see beyond our doom, i.e.,
God's love.[37] Sin is, therefore, approached
from the side of grace. If understood from this
perspective, then the final word must be that of
triumph, that of new creation.

From this point of view of grace, sin is
seen as the totality over against the totality
of grace, and sin is seen as the fundamental
problem at the root of man's relation to God.
Sin is seen as a power over human existence
controlling and shaping a man's life and being.
The manifestation of this sinful state is really
irrelevant for what is ultimately significant
is the "robbery of God."

> Clearly, --- and this lies already in the
> Word "fall" --- God is here deserted and
> denied by men; He suffers and is robbed.
> Sin is robbing God of what He is: and
> because it is a robbing of God, sin is
> essentially the appearance in the world
> of a power-like-God.[38]

This robbery becomes apparent in our efforts to blur,
by means of religion and otherwise, the diastasis,
in our apparent deification of man. In this respect
we devote ourselves to a "No-God" of this world.
Thus man by manifesting his ungodliness and un-
righteousness in a damaged relationship takes to
heart the statement, "eritis sicut Deus."[39]

We may see then that sin is a world power
conditioning human existence; we see that death
is the way in which the NO points up and exposes
the imprisonment of man within his own will. It
is this judgment that emits light and makes clear

the relationship of God to man and man to God.

> Death never occurs but it calls attention
> to our participation in the Life of God
> and to that relationship of His which is
> not broken by sin. The thought of Life
> and of God is stirred in us by death ---
> by the reality of death, not by our
> experience of it.[40]

Furthermore, man's sin reveals that he is bound by
God's judgment and his temporality by eternity. In
other words, Barth contrasts religion and grace.[41]
The vitality of man in the sphere of religion
tries to press forward and tries to cross over
the boundary making themselves in effect what God
ought to be to them.

> ...transforming time into eternity, and
> therefore eternity into time, they stretch
> themselves beyond the boundary of death,
> rob the Unknown God of what He is, push
> themselves into His domain, and depress
> Him to their own level....They make Him a
> thing of this world, and set Him in the
> midst of other things.[42]

But, on the other hand, grace means that God
reckons man's whole existence to be His and claims
it for Himself. Grace is the power of God that
can never, actively or passively, be associated
with the possibilities of man. It is the divine
possibility for men alongside other human possibilities.[43] Modern theology had done or tried to
do just this --- to convert grace into a human
possibility.

(2)

Another dominant theme, as we have seen from
our consideration of the Blumhardts, is eschatology.
This teaching that the supernatural Kingdom invades
the world in Jesus Christ opened up new avenues for
Karl Barth. Barth's earliest position was that of
a "timeless eschatology." That is: the end of
history is not to be interpreted as an end within

-23-

time as we know it, for no end within time can be a
real or complete end. The end is also the beginning,
and so the nearness of the end is interpreted as
the transcendental relation of the present to its
origin in the eternal.

Barth criticized himself on this point and
changed his view. He took the eschatological tension
out of an eternity/time dialectic and placed in its
stead a tension between the new time in reconciliation
and the old time of "Fall" world which exists in
contradiction to God. It is seen in the shift that
his theology took from the position of totaliter
aliter to his ultimate and mature Christological
view. Be that as it may, he deals with the problem
of eschatology at a time when the "uneschatological
gospel" was at its peak.

(3)

Karl Barth's name has been linked with dialectical theology, which is inescapable, because it is
thinking about God from the center of man without
ever seeking to usurp God's own standpoint. It is a
dangerous venture, but it is also necessary, at
least for Barth. It is dialogical thinking in which
man remains man but in which he meets God, listens
to Him, answers Him and speaks of Him in such a way
that at every point he gives God the glory. Here
we may see the influence of Soren Kierkegaard and
his conceptions of "paradox" and "indirect communication."

The primary factor giving rise to the concept
of dialectical thinking was in the attempt to do
justice to the revelation of God and to the witness
of scripture. Neo-Protestantism had not taken this
seriously and Barth had to shatter the basic axiom
of immanent continuity between man and God, but
in doing so he did not desire to sacrifice either
of the two poles of thought: God or man. Therefore,
they had to be held in dialectical relation, and
until the NO in the relationship had completed
its work, there can be no positive fruitful affirmation.
Consequently, dialectical theology is the attempt

to affirm both God and man and still suspend full
positive account of their relation to one another.[44]
Here we see the NO derived perhaps with the aid of
Overbeck's "eschatological death," "the Wholly
Other," "the infinite qualitative distinction,"
of Kierkegaard, and the vertical invasion of the
Blumhardts fashioning a YES all to some degree
showing their influence. And we see it continued
in Barth with creations of his own: "krisis,"
"boundary," etc. In reviewing this picture
himself, Barth admits that his reactions may have
been excessive, but that it was nevertheless
necessary. Indeed, "everything that even from
afar smelt of mysticism and morals, of pietism
and of romanticism or even idealism, how suspect
it was and how strictly prohibited or confined in
the straitjacket of restrictions that sounded
prohibitive."[45] Completely correct? Perhaps
not, but he asks, "Was there not foundation for
standing Schleiermacher on his head to make God
great?"[46]

This was the way that Barth faced the fundamental problem of thinking about God. For it is
man who thinks, man who asks searching questions
about God, man who is hungry to know about God, to
speak about Him and make judgments about Him; but
when that man stands face to face with God, he
discovers that he stands at the point of God's
judgment and it is God who speaks to him and questions him. Man begins by investigating God but discovers that God is all the time investigating
him --- and when he tries to express that, theologically, he finds himself, as it were, at a grammarian's
funeral --- for God is always indissolubly Subject ---
and all he can do is to stammer weakly "yes" and "no"
in very fragmentary utterances.

In his essay, The Humanity of God, Barth states,
"What began forcibly to press itself upon us about
forty years ago was not so much the humanity of
God as His deity --- a God absolutely unique in His
relation to man and the world, overpoweringly
lofty and distant, strange, yes even wholly other."[47]
And so Barth began to trace his own theological
development. It seems obvious as we look back that

-25-

the great devestation that Barth employed was
necessary if it was to be heard at all, but even so
he felt that it was correct and he appeals for us
to read the doctrine of Ernst Troeltsch and the
dogmatics of Ludeman and see for ourselves. Furthermore, he does not feel that his ultimate position
is anything like a retreat or an abandonment, but
is, with a new beginning and attack, saying that
which was also said before but now with a new
precision, said so much better.[48]

    These early thoughts constitute the presupposi-
tions of Barth's theology in his mature years and
consequently must also be considered at both ends
of the Barthian spectrum. G. C. Berkouwer views the
picture as follows: "To a certain extent we can
agree with Vogel that in the first phase of Barth's
theological development the emphasis falls on grace
in the judgment while the later development showed
that he was more concerned to manifest grace in the
judgment."[49] This statement seems to be true as far
as it goes but it should be qualified to the extent
that we can legitimately say that all the ingredients
of Barth's theology were possibly present and
through his tireless efforts of constant questioning
and reflection different emphases have become manifest.
For it seems that one would hardly expect Barth to
speak of the "Humanity Of God" in his earlier period,
as he himself has already stated.[50] However, because
he was the man he was and continued to question
and be self-critical, as well as listening to
others, one would not expect that his theology would
stand still. It seems that if we look very generally,
including his early thought, we can see it move
through an anthropocentric stage (19th Century con-
sciousness-theology) to what we may call a theo-
centric stage (characterized by the Wholly Other,
etc.) and finally to a Christological stage with
Jesus Christ as central, as being the Mediator
between God and man, as God for man, representing
man, making satisfaction and interceding, thereby
guaranteeing God's free grace and at the same time
guaranteeing to God man's gratitude. Thus he
establishes in His Person the justice of God vis-
a-vis man and also the justice of man before God.

CHAPTER 1 NOTES

1. Karl Barth, "Liberal Theology: Some Alternatives,"
The Hibbert Journal, April 1961, quoted from Karl
Barth: An Introduction To His Early Theology 1910-
1931, by T. F. Torrance, p. 33.

2. Karl Barth, Epistle to the Romans, translated
by Edwyn C. Hoskyns from the 6th edition (Oxford:
University Press, 1935), cf., p. 254, "May God never
relieve us from questioning...they must never cease
for one moment."

3. E. G., the lecture in The Word of God and the Word
of Man, "The Strange New World Within the Bible"
(New York: Harper and Row, 1957), pp. 28-50.

4. Karl Barth, "On Systematic Theology," The Scottish
Journal of Theology, Volume 14, No. 3, September,
1961, p. 225.

5. Barth, Romans, p. 239.

6. Karl Barth, The Humanity of God (Richmond: John
Knox Press, 1960), p. 39.

7. Ibid., pp. 39-40.

8. Barth, The Word of God and the Word of Man, pp. 14-19.

9. Barth, Romans, p. 238.

10. Ibid.

11. Ibid., pp. 183-184. That text reads: "Law came
in, to increase the trespass, but where sin increased,
grace abounded all the more." (RSV)

12. Ibid., pp. 183-185.

13. Karl Barth, Die Lehre vom Worte Gottes: Prole-
gomena zur Christlichen Dogmatik (Munchen: Chr.
Kaiser Verlag, 1927), p. lx., translated by Paul
Lehmann in his article "The Changing Course of a
Corrective Theology," in Theology Today, Volume
XIII, No. 3, October 1956, p. 334.

-27-

14. Karl Barth, God, Gospel and Grace, translated by James S. McNab, Scottish Journal of Theology Occasional Papers No. 8 (Edinburgh: Oliver and Boyd, 1959), p. 57f.

15. Barth, The Humanity of God, p. 38.

16. Karl Barth, "The Need of Christian Preaching," in The Word of God and the Word of Man, p. 100.

17. Barth, Romans, p. 3.

18. Karl Barth, Theology and Church (London: SCM Press, Ltd., 1962), p. 57f.

19. Ibid., p. 69.

20. Letter of Karl Barth to Eduard Thurneysen, April 20, 1920 in Revolutionary Theology in the Making: Barth-Thurneysen Correspondence 1914-1925, translated by James D. Smart (Richmond: John Knox Press, 1964), p. 50.

21. Quoted by Arthur Wiser in his introduction to Action in Waiting (Rifton, N.Y., Plough Publishing House, 1969), p. 11.

22. I Corinthians 15:42-43. (RSV) Barth cogently develops this point in Dogmatics in Outline (New York: Philosophical Library, 1947), p. 122.

23. Kierkegaard as quoted by Karl Barth in Romans, p. 279.

24. Ibid., p. 10.

25. Barth, The Word of God and the Word of Man, p. 206.

26. Barth, Die Christliche Dogmatik, pp. 456-457.

27. John Godsey, How I Changed My Mind (Richmond: John Knox Press, 1966), p. 32-33.

28. Paul Tillich, "The Present Theological Situation in the Light of the Continental European Development," Theology Today, No. 6, October, 1949, p. 302.

29. Barth, Romans, p. 278; cf., pp. 395, 440.

30. Barth, The Humanity of God, pp. 40-41.

31. George S. Hendry, "Barth for Beginners," Theology Today, Volume XIX, July, 1962, pp. 267-268.

32. Barth, The Word of God and the Word of Man, p. 286.

33. Barth, Romans, p. 45.

34. G. C. Berkouwer, The Triumph of Grace in the Theology of Karl Barth (Grand Rapids: Eerdmans Publishing Co., 1956), pp. 38-39.

35. Barth, Romans, p. 215.

36. Barth, The Word of God and the Word of Man, pp. 136-182.

37. Ibid., p. 169.

38. Barth, Romans, p. 177.

39. Ibid., p. 167f.

40. Ibid., p. 170.

41. Ibid., p. 244.

42. Ibid., p. 216.

43. Ibid.

44. Barth, The Word of God and the Word of Man, p. 206ff.

45. Barth, The Humanity of God, p. 43.

46. Ibid. (Emphasis added)

47. Ibid., p. 37.

48. Ibid., pp. 41-42.

49. Berkouwer, <u>The Triumph of Grace in the Theology of Karl Barth</u>, p. 49.

50. Barth, <u>The Humanity of God</u>, p. 38.

CHAPTER II

THE NATURE OF THE PROBLEM OF THE TRINITY

It is generally assumed that the major problem
in trinitarian doctrine concerns the way in which
God can be one "person," yet three. This is,
certainly, a real issue, but it is not the most
basic one. There are others who have felt that it
is the place of the Holy Spirit that is most difficult to explain and to understand. This also is
a very significant question, but it is also secondary.
Rather, the most fundamental issue, the most basic
problem is the distinction that is to be made
between the Father and the Son. All trinitarian
theology ultimately hinges on this distinction,
and this distinction, as we are all well aware,
has been variously interpreted in the history of
Christian thought.[1]

Because the Christian Church upheld the Jewish
belief in the unity of God, the belief in Christ's
divinity raised serious problems. Why should we
posit two terms, Father and Son, in the Godhead?
How could the Father and the Son be God and yet
be one God? In what way do they differ? The
answer that is given appears to be relatively
simple. Theologians have generally maintained
that the Father and the Son differ in that the Son
is derived from, or "begotten" from, the Father.
But the difficulty is, when we have made this
assertion, what have we really said? What does
this really mean? In what sense may we say the
one is begotten of the other? Strictly speaking,
if we couch the problem in terms of the Father
and Son alone, it is bi-nitarian. But whether the
problem is binitarian or trinitarian in form, the
crucial issue that manifests itself is the relationship of the Father and the Son, because the
problem, in fact, would not have been of practical
importance if there had been no Incarnation, i.e.,
if the Word had not been made flesh there would
have been no stumbling block for Jewish monotheism
or foolishness for Greek philosophers.[2] Further,
it may be asked, "Is the Holy Spirit also God,
and if so, how could God be three and one?" In
these three names: Father, Son and Holy Spirit
we have the summation of the New Testament message
and the postulation of the problem of the Trinity.
Whether or not this was in the minds of the New

Testament writers, as Professor Arthur W. Wainwright seems to suggest, we may, at least, certainly agree that their witness led to the subsequest theological formulation of the trinitarian dogma.

For our purposes, i.e., in delineating the problem, we shall confine our discussion to the distinction between the Father and the Son, which we see as the basic distinction. In the Old Testament we discover God in distinction from those creatures with whom He has a unique relation, those who respond to His call, and who, recognizing their creaturely dependence upon Him, yield themselves to the vocation He gives them. This idea of the intimate relation between God as the heavenly Father and man as His Son, was given new and richer meaning in the life and teaching of Jesus of Nazareth. For Him was reserved the deepest intimacy of this relationship, for He, in a unique way, is the Son of God, chosen for a special vocation and doing of the will of God.

He is so marked at His baptism:

And there came a voice from heaven, saying,
Thou art my beloved Son, with Thee I am well-pleased;[3]

And His transfiguration:

And a cloud overshadowed them, and a voice
came out of the cloud. This is my beloved
Son; listen to Him.[4]

Yet unique or close as this relation is, it is not a relation of equality or identity.

This is taken a step further by the Apostle Paul, for whom the term Son of God takes on a new meaning. The risen Jesus is God's Son by nature, while men are only sons of God by adoption.[5] He is a heavenly being "in the form of God,"[6] God's express image and the "first-born of all creation."[7] The implication here is that there is some sort of distinction within the Godhead itself. While Paul

-34-

never reaches an overt expression of this, it becomes quite clear in John: Jesus is the Word, the
Logos become incarnate. "In the beginning was
the Word, and the Word was with God, and the Word
was God....And the Word became flesh and dwelt
among us...."[8] But what does this mean? It means
that the Word of God whereby He comes into relationship with the world, whereby He creates and
reveals Himself.

Therein lies the real substance of the problem
of the doctrine of the Trinity. For in this momentous idea, which rests upon the assumption that God
is absolutely transcendent, remote, indivisible,
unknowable and complete in Himself, and yet related
to the world, we discover the distinction about the
paradoxical nature of God, i.e., absolutely above
and beyond and yet at the same time near and immanent.
Professor Cyril Richardson points out that such
statements must be made on "philosophical no less
than religious grounds."[9] That is to say, philosophically we have somehow to apply to God the
idea of the absolute --- to say that He is alone,
single, incomparable and so forth; for there cannot
be two absolutes since the one would qualify the
other. Yet we have also to say that He comes into
relationship. He creates, and by so doing, the
magic spell of His absolute nature is broken. The
one is now involved in the many. The remoteness,
the self-sufficiency and the absolute transcendence
of God are overcome in His creating and being related
to His creatures. The Christian doctrines of Creation
and the Incarnation demand that we say these apparently
contradictory things. He is absolute, yet He is
also Creator, Incarnate and Redeemer. The expression
"Son of God" in the Apostle Paul and the "Logos" or
"Word" in John are expressions of this belief,
i.e., that God is absolutely transcendent and yet
related to His creatures. In this connection,
Professor George S. Hendry states: "Paul consistently
distinguishes between God and Christ, and he never
ascribes to God the historical actions and experiences of which Christ was the subject. But
since those actions and experiences derive their

-35-

evangelical significance from the fact that God was
the ultimate author of them, Christ may be described
as the self-expression or self-objectification of
God in history."[10] Thus that God is beyond and
yet related is the essence of the distinction between
the Father and the Son and is, as such, the most
important problem in trinitarian theology. From
this it is quite apparent that the theological
doctrines of the Trinity and the Incarnation are
so interwoven that it is impossible to study the
doctrine of the Trinity without serious consideration being given to the doctrine of the Incarnation.
It is important to see this clearly for the reper-
cussions of the incarnation, from a doctrinal point
of view, are seen and felt throughout all trinitarian
thinking.

Nevertheless, while we may say that this self-
differentiation in God, manifest in Jesus Christ,
is the most basic, most elemental problem concerning
trinitarian dogma, and that without it there would
seemingly be no problem at all, we may not say that
it is the only problem. At least two other questions lend their presence to the difficulties of
this problem of the Trinity. There is the question
of the relationship between the Holy Spirit and
Christ and between the Holy Spirit and the Father.
Furthermore, there is the problem of the Three-in-
oneness and the One-in-threeness which causes con-
siderable difficulty,[11] i.e., the problem of unity
in Trinity and Trinity in unity.

It has come to be a common reproach that when
the Christian Church came to formulate its faith
in the era of the great Councils, it introduced
subtleties and complexities that go beyond anything
to be found in the New Testament scriptures. The
main occasion of this reproach has always been
that it was only by these careful elaborations that
the Church was able to guard against the perversion
of the essential elements of the New Testament
faith by heretics. This is neither completely true
nor completely false. As Dr. George Hendry has
lucidly pointed out, while such a reproach may be
leveled at what the church had to say about the deity

of Christ, "it ...can certainly not be leveled at
what the Church had to say about the Holy Spirit.
Rather the contrary. If the Church went considerably
beyond the New Testament in defining the doctrine
of the Person of Christ, it fell considerably short
of the New Testament in defining the doctrine of
the Holy Spirit."12 We would therefore call attention to the fact that the problem is seriously
present in trinitarian thought, even though it may
not have been a major consideration for the New
Testament writers and the early Fathers, as
Wainwright seems to suggest.13

     At this point a further word must be said
about the "Biblical" doctrine of the Trinity. It
is generally agreed that the doctrine of the
Trinity is not found in the New Testament. At
the same time, it is more commonly recognized
that it has been in the past that the New Testament
contains the materials out of which the doctrine
of the Trinity took shape; and these are to be
found not so much in the texts in which the names
of the three "persons" occur together, as in the
outlines of a trinitarian pattern which can be
discerned, especially in the thought of John or
Paul. But it was not, indeed, until considerably
later than the New Testament that the full implications of this type of thinking were seen and a more
adequate way of expressing it in the ternal
generations of the Son was elaborated.14

     In his comprehensive treatise on the doctrine
of the Trinity articulated in Volume I/1 of his
Church Dogmatics under the heading of the "doctrine
of the Word of God," Karl Barth comes to grips
with each of the problems we have presented here in
outline. In approaching these difficulties and
problems, he grounds his conception of the doctrine
of the Trinity in revelation. By taking this
particular theological stance he feels that he is
properly representing the understanding and positions
of the Biblical writers. In this way the doctrine
of the Trinity is not conceived of as an indirect
consequence of the revelation of God in Christ nor
as an intellectual synthesis subsequent to other

more primary and independent affirmations. Rather,
Barth conceives of the doctrine of the Trinity
as the very center of the faith. Therefore, his
conception of the Trinity may be seen correctly,
as an analysis, an interpretation, i.e., as the
immediate implicate of revelation. It shall be
our endeavor in our presentation, at this point,
to analyze Karl Barth's answer to the questions
of the Trinity. Moreover, in so doing, it is only
prudent for us to be well aware, as was Karl
Barth, and hopefully anyone who reflects upon
God's activity or contemplates His divine nature,
in order to understand more fully, that we are
attempting to express the inexpressible, and to
comprehend the incomprehensible, for we are finite
creatures and _finitum_ _non_ _capax_ _infiniti_. Nevertheless, we must attempt this impossibility and
the only way we may do so is in terms of the
Anselmic formula: _fides_ _quarens_ _intellectum_.

CHAPTER 2 NOTES

1. We do not mean to minimize either of these very significant and important questions; rather it is suggested that without the problem raised by the incarnation, these other problems most likely would not have occurred.

2. Cyril C. Richardson, The Doctrine of the Trinity (New York: Abington Press: 1958), pp. 19-20; Cf., Robert S. Franks, The Doctrine of the Trinity (London: Gerald Duckworth & Co., Ltd., 1953), pp. 2-3; Cf., Arthur W. Wainwright, The Trinity in the New Testament (London: S.P.C.K., 1962), p. 3.

3. Mark 1:11 (RSV)

4. Mark 9:7 (RSV)

5. Galatians 4:4ff. (RSV)

6. Philippians 2:6 (RSV)

7. Colossians 1:15 (RSV)

8. John 1:1; 1:14 (RSV)

9. Richardson, op. cit., p. 21.

10. George S. Hendry, The Holy Spirit in Christian Theology, (Philadelphia: The Westminster Press, 1956), pp. 33-34; emphasis added.

11. Indeed Barth states, with respect to these concepts, that we do nothing more than affirm, in the form of a conflation of the two, each (Church Dogmatics, I/1, p. 425.)

12. George S. Hendry, The Holy Spirit in Christian Theology, p. 37; Cf., G. L. Prestige, God in Patristic Thought (London: William Heinman Ltd., 1936), p. 79f.

13. Wainwright, op. cit., p. 249.

14. Franks, op. cit., pp. 4-5. Wainwright writes in his work, The Trinity in the New Testament, that the problem of the Trinity is raised in the New Testament; and that an attempt is made to answer it. Thus, he maintains, insofar as doctrine is an answer to a problem, the doctrine of the Trinity emerges in the New Testament. He argues further that not only is the problem of the Trinity in the New Testament but that it is also present in the minds of the writers as well. While we may find ourselves somewhat in accord with the first part of Wainwright's statement, the second part goes beyond the evidence. As J. A. T. Knight points out in his article in the Scottish Journal of Theology, "A Biblical Approach to the Doctrine of the Trinity," we must remember that the dogma of the Trinity that is dealt with by the systematic theologian is not a biblical dogma as such; it is rather just an interpretation of what we find in the Bible (pg.1.)." Knight maintains that the Biblical aspect is concerned with the latter part of the statement, i.e., what we find, leaving the interpretation or analysis to others. It is imperative that we be fully aware of this distinction when considering the "theological" doctrine of the Trinity.

CHAPTER III

KARL BARTH'S CONCEPT OF REVELATION

Having outlined, very briefly, what constitutes the essential nature of the problem of the doctrine of the Trinity, i.e., the distinction between the Father and the Son, we shall now proceed to examine how this problem is treated in the theology of Karl Barth. The problem of the distinction between the Father and the Son necessarily involves the problem of revelation, for, as we stated in the previous chapter, without the incarnation, without the Word becoming flesh, which is the summa of the Christian revelation, this difficulty would not have arisen.

Presenting a discussion of the way in which Karl Barth conceives of the doctrine of the Trinity necessarily involves a consideration of how he conceives of revelation since we shall be maintaining that his position with respect to the Trinity is that the doctrine is the immediate implicate of revelation, i.e., an analysis of the statement "God reveals Himself." To these matters we now turn confining ourselves to the area of the threefold form of the Word of God and the knowability of the Word of God in this chapter and a specific consideration, in some detail, of the doctrine of the Trinity in the succeeding chapter.

A. THE WORD OF GOD IN ITS THREEFOLD FORM

The Word of God, according to Barth, has a threefold form, namely, the proclaimed, the written and the revealed Word of God. He states his thesis in the following terms: "The presupposition which makes proclamation to be proclamation and therewith the Church to be the Church, is the Word of God. It attests itself in Holy Scripture in the word of the prophets and apostles, to whom it was originally and once for all uttered through God's revelation."[1] Let us, therefore, consider this threefold form of the Word of God in the order stated above.

1. The Word of God Proclaimed

Proclamation, according to Barth, is human speech in and through which God Himself speaks, as a king by

-43-

the mouth of a herald and which is also intended
to be heard and received as such, i.e., heard and
received in faith. Such speech is speech concerning God and takes place within the bounds of
the Church. Thus by

> proclamation of the 'Word of God' we are
> to understand withal, primarily and deci-
> sively, <u>preaching</u> and the sacraments; with
> regard to the latter which as verba visibilia
> in actions, belong to a special order, the
> main thing will likewise be the oral pro-
> clamation accompanying them, the 'doctrine'
> of the sacraments which is significant for
> the meaning of their administration in
> vogue at the time.[2]

Furthermore, Barth states:

> The language about God to be found in the
> Church is meant to be proclamation, so far
> as it is directed towards man in the form
> of preaching and sacrament, with the claim
> and in an atmosphere of expectation that is in
> accordance with its commission it has to
> tell him the Word of God to be heard in
> faith.[3]

And,

> The Word of God is Himself in the proclama-
> tion of the Church of Jesus Christ. In so
> far as God gives the Church the commission to
> speak about Him, and the Church discharges
> this commission, it is God Himself who de-
> clares His revelation in His witnesses. The
> proclamation of the Church is pure doctrine
> when the human word spoken in it in con-
> firmation of the biblical witness to reve-
> lation offers and creates obedience to the
> Word of God.[4]

But not all speech of the Church concerning God is
intended as such proclamation. For example: prayer
and singing and confessions of faith are intended
as a sacrifice or response to God rather than as
"proclamation." Furthermore, the social work

-44-

of the Church, the instruction of its youth and its
theology are other elements that are not primarily
intended as "proclamation." The speech in the first
is directed primarily to God and not to men; that
of the second prepares for the understanding of the
proclamation, while theology presupposes and reflects
upon proclamation, although Barth admits that it
may itself also become proclamation.[5]

In distinction from these, the Church's speech
which is expressly intended as proclamation is that
which is directed to man with the definite claim,
and attended by the definite expression, that it is
to speak God's Word to them, Which speech is this?
Or which functions of the Church are directly
concerned with proclamation? Barth responds:
preaching and the sacraments! God can speak to
us by any method He chooses, but the Church as we
know it has a commission to proclaim God's speech
in only one instance. This commission, according
to the testimony of the Bible, comes to us from
Jesus Christ and is executed by preaching and the
sacraments when these are rightly exercised.[6]

In a contributory essay on "Revelation" to
a volume of the same name, Barth refers to these
elements as tokens of revelation. That is: because Holy Scripture is itself a token of revelation, there exists in the Church as further tokens
of revelation: proclamation, i.e., preaching and
the sacraments. Preaching is defined as the utterance
whose subject and creative form is the Biblical
witness; and as such it is a proclaiming of Jesus
Christ's action as present ever anew.[7] Or as Karl
Barth himself expresses it:

> (It is) the attempt, essayed by one called
> thereto in the Church, to express in his
> own words in the form of an exposition of
> a portion of the Biblical testimony to
> revelation, and to make comprehensible to
> men of his day, the promise of God's reve-
> lation, reconciliation and calling, as they
> are to be expected here and now.[8]

The sacrament, on the other hand, is defined as a
symbolic act consummated in the sense of, and in
accordance with, the Biblical witness. It is the

confirmation of the action of Jesus as something
which has taken place for us, and happened to us,
once and for all. Thus preaching, and the sacraments too, are in different ways, but still in this
difference at one, mutually explanatory tokens of
revelation.[9] Neither of these tokens, preaching
or sacrament, can be dispensed with for this representation must consist in testimony true to
revelation as present as well as once for all.
On the other hand, neither preaching nor sacrament
is effective of itself; but both are effective
through the power of the revelation which they
attest and through that alone.

As these definitions indicate, preaching and
the sacraments are intended as "proclamation."
Whether or not they are such, however, depends
upon the Word of God itself, i.e., "the presupposition of this actual event is the Word of God."[10]
Between this central concept of proclamation lie
four decisive connections. First: that the Word of
God is the commission on the basis of whose given-
ness the proclamation must rest in order to be real
proclamation. Human motives cannot and should not
be eliminated here, but no proclamation is real
proclamation unless, besides these human motives,
this commission is also present. Barth makes
the point in these words:

> No proclamation but also depends upon
> such present human motives calling for
> validation. But no proclamation is
> real proclamation, so far as it does
> not also and beyond all that rest upon
> the commission, a commission we cannot
> take unto ourselves or take for granted
> in any way, which we can simply just re-
> ceive and possess in the act of recep-
> tion, which simply touches, elevates and
> defines us and the entire word of our
> motivations from without, as a behest
> that comes to us in an unforseen way....
> Real proclamation thus means the Word of
> God preached, and the Word of God preached
> means, in this first and outmost circle,
> man's language about God on the basis of
> an indication by God Himself fundamentally

-46-

transcending all human causation, and so
devoid of all human basis, merely occurring
as a fact and requiring to be acknowledged.[11]

Second: The Word of God is the Gegenstand
(object) which must be given to proclamation in
order that it may be real proclamation. This
Gegenstand (object) must become a Gegenstand of
human perception in order to be proclaimed; but in
so far as it is really proclaimed it is not at all
a Gegenstand of human perception, but an object that
presents and places itself over against all other
objects. Thus in this second relation, real proclamation means God's Word preached, and God's
Word preached means, in this second relation,
man's language about God on the basis of His self-
objectification which is neither present nor pre-
dictable, but is real solely in the freedom of His
grace, in virtue of which He from time to time
wills to be the object of this language.[12]

Third: "The Word of God is the judgment in
virtue of which proclamation can alone become a
real proclamation,"[13] that is, it is God's own
judgment concerning the truth of the proclamation.
It is out of our hands; it handles itself. Thus,
in this third sense, real proclamation can never
pass into our control and in view of the object
proclaimed and the subject proclaiming, is true
language and therefore language to be listened to
and language which rightly demands obedience.

Finally, the Word of God is the event itself
in which the proclamation becomes real proclamation,
and this is, according to Barth, the decisive
factor. Even from all the points of view already
elucidated, i.e., the commission, the object and
the judgment, the realization of proclamation
might be regarded as merely external accidental
characteristics, a sort of vesture or illumination
of an event, which as such still remained exclu-
sively the event of the will and execution of the
man proclaiming.[14] But real proclamation does not
consist in the volition and execution of the man
proclaiming, with his completely conditioned state
and his utterly problematic nature being omitted.
It is as Christ became true man and remains so to
all eternity that real proclamation becomes an
event on the human level of all other events. To

put it another way, human speech about God is not
set aside, but exalted by the fact that God Himself
speaks in it and through it. When these four elements
or these four relations are realized we have what
Barth calls the proclaimed Word of God.

2. The Word of God Written

We may now ask, in Barth's conception of the
matter, how is this proclaimed Word of God related
to the written Word of God? Barth asserts: "We
speak...of a realized proclamation, of a God
proclaimed in the Church, on the basis that God's
Word has already been spoken, that revelation has
already taken place. We therefore speak in recollection."[15] This recollection is seen to be
identical with the discovery and fresh appropriation
of a long hidden, forgotten and unused part, namely,
the timeless essential state of man in his relationship to the eternal or absolute.[16] And the specific
revelation that we recollect is that reported in
the Bible. In other words, the proclamation of the
Church is related to a concrete exterior standard,
without which it could not exist and for which no
substitute is thinkable.

There is both a phenomenal similarity and
dissimilarity between Church proclamation and the
canon of Holy Scripture. This phenomenal similarity consists in the fact that obviously even
in Holy Scripture we are dealing with Scripture
not in the primary but in the secondary sense:
for it itself is the deposit of PROCLAMATION made
in the past by the mouth of man. Thus there is one
genus. Jeremiah and Paul stand at the beginning
and the preacher at the end of one and the same
series. On the other hand, there is also an un-
likeness in order between Holy Scripture and proclamation today. There is a fundamental distinction
to be made concerning the words of the prophets
and the apostles above all other words spoken later
in the Church and words which need to be spoken today.
Thus Holy Scripture constitutes the basis and
standard of present-day proclamation. The fact,
however, that this standard comes to the Church
in written form enables the Church to distinguish

-48-

it from its own reflections and ever to return to it for correction.

The further question which is to be asked is: how does it come about that the prophetic and apostolic Word in particular takes up this normative position over against the Church and her proclamation? In other words, what makes the Bible of the Old and New Testaments and no other document into the canon? Why must the Church's recollection of God's past revelation always have the Bible in particular as its concrete object? In answer to this question Barth replies, quite simply, and without apology, that it makes itself such. It is the canon since it has impressed itself, and constantly does impress itself, as such upon men.

The Bible is the concrete object of the Church's recollection of the revelation of God which has taken place, since, as a matter of fact, it is the promise of future divine revelation, that can make the Church feel the obligatory character of its proclamation and can give it joy and courage in the execution of it. Why this is so, we cannot specify, although we can, subsequent to its occurrence, exegetically, indicate in what this impression of itself consists by considering its unique content. Scripture is the word of men, who longed for, expected, hoped for this "Immanuel," and finally saw, heard and handled it in Jesus Christ. And it assures us by its witness and proclamation that its message is for us. Therefore, whoever

> hears its word in such a way that he grasps its promise and says <u>Yea</u> to it, believes. And this very grasp and affirmation of the promise, Immanuel with sinners! In the word of prophets and apostles, is the Church's actual faith. In such faith she reminds herself of God's revelation already past, and in such faith she expects the future ....revelation still outstanding, she reminds herself of the incarnation of the eternal Word and the reconciliation that took place in Him, and she awaits the coming of Jesus Christ and her own redemption from the power of evil.[18]

-49-

It is thus in virtue of this its content that Scripture imposes itself and is an imperative and a
final word that cannot be exchanged or classed
with another.[19]

As such a source and standard of present day
proclamation, Scripture, also, is a form of the
Word of God for Barth, and that as in the case of
real proclamation, as a matter of divine occurence.
In this event the human word of prophets and apostles represents the Word of God Himself, exactly
in the way in which the Word of God is to become
the human word of the preacher today, namely, as
man's word with God's commission to us behind it,
man's word to which God has given Himself as object,
man's word which is acknowledged and accepted by
God as good and in which God's own language to us
is an event. That the Bible speaks to us concerning the promise, that the prophets and apostles
succeed in saying to us what they have to say, that
the word of the Bible impresses us, that is a
matter of God's, and not our, decision, of grace
and not of works. The Bible is God's Word in so far
as He lets His Word, in so far as God speaks through
it. Hence the proposition "The Bible is the Word
of God" is a confession of faith, a proposition
made by faith which hears God Himself speaking in
the human word of the Bible. Aside from this event,
aside from God's action by which Scripture becomes,
repeatedly, the Word of God, it is not the Word of
God.[20] As Barth put it:

The Bible therefore becomes God's Word
in this event, and it is to its being in
this becoming that the tiny word "is"
relates, in the statement that the Bible
is God's Word. It does not become God's
Word because we accord it faith, but, of
course, because it becomes Revelation
for us. But its becoming revelation for
us beyond all our faith, its being the
Word of God also against our unbelief, we
can, of course, allow to be true and
confess as true in us and for us only in
faith, in faith against unbelief, in the
faith in which we look away from our faith

-50-

and unbelief to the act of God, but in faith
and not in unbelief. And therefore precisely
not in abstraction from the act of God, in
virtue of which the Bible must from time to
time become His Word to us.[21]

3. The Revealed Word of God

In treating of the revealed Word of God, Barth
says that the revelation to which the Biblical
witnesses point differs formally from the word
of these witnesses as a happening differs from the
best report of it. This difference, however, is
inconsiderable, says Barth, when placed alongside
the fact that this revelation concerns the coming
of Jesus Christ, that is, God's own, literal and
now immediately, spoken Word. In other words,
revelation, as Barth uses the term, is originally
and immediately what the Bible and the proclamation
of the Church are in a derived and mediate way:
The Word of God.[22] Viewed in this way revelation
takes place as an event, when and where the
Scripture becomes God's Word, i.e., when and where
the word of the Bible functions as the word of a
witness or when and where we also succeed in seeing
and hearing what the writers saw and heard. Where
the Word of God is an event, therefore, revelation
and the Bible are one in fact:

Revelation does in fact not differ from
the Person of Jesus Christ, and again does
not differ from the reconciliation that took
place in Him. To say "revelation" is to say
"The Word became flesh."[23]

It is the divine decision that confirms, verifies
and fulfills the Bible and the proclamation when
it uses them. It is the Word of God that the Bible
and proclamation become. Thus

revelation engenders the Scripture which
attests it, as the commission, the "burden"
laid upon the prophets and apostles, as
the object which introduces itself per-
sonally into the scheme over against them,
as the judge at once and the guarantor of

the truth of their language, as the event
of inspiration in which they become speakers
and writers of the Word of God.[24]

This revelation, Barth maintains, has actually
and conclusively taken place once and for all, and
it has taken place in the midst of human history,
and as a part of this history, but not as parts
of history usually take place. It is, namely, not
in need of completion and continuation; it does
not point beyond itself nor strive towards a far
away end; it is not open to exegesis nor to the
least addition or substraction; it is not capable
of changing its form; but in the midst of the
stream of becoming it is "das nur in sich selbst
bewegete Sein," in the midst of the sea of the un-
completed happening, the fulfilled time, which is
identical with Jesus Christ. There is no higher
act by which revelation is to be founded or from
which it is to be deduced. It is a condition
that conditions everything, without itself,
however, being conditioned. In his article,
"Revelation," Barth puts the point in this way:

> Jesus Christ is the revelation because He
> is the grace of God made manifest to us
> --- grace in the full sense of the con-
> ception. Revelation means that God, without
> ceasing to be God, was made man, 'flesh.'
> Flesh means man like us in our finitude,
> infirmity and helplessness that charac-
> terizes our human life and results from our
> utter distance from God. Revelation means
> grace. Grace means condescension. Condes-
> cension means being made man. Being made
> man means being made flesh. Jesus Christ is
> all that. And that, and that alone is
> Revelation.[25]

This deus dixit, to which there are no analogies, is
the revelation attested in Scripture. It is an
unveiling of that which is veiled and everything
that differs from it is a veiling, a hiddenness of
that which is veiled.

According to all that has been said, revelation
is, therefore, immediately, what the Bible and proclamation are derivatively and mediately, i.e.,
God's Word (cf. pp. 32-40). This revelation,
according to Barth, produces the Scriptures: as
the commission to the prophets and apostles, as
the Gegenstand that presents itself to them, as
the judge and surety of the truth of their speech,
and as the occurrence of the inspiration in which
they become speakers and writers of the Word of God.
It constitutes the proclamation of the Old Testament as the Word of Fulfillment.

In this understanding of revelation, as we
have already indicated, Church proclamation and
Scripture must from time to time become the Word
of God. However, a word of explanation must be
said about this notion. It has to do, says Barth,
"not with human experience (as if our being
affected by this event and our attitude toward it
could be constitutive of its reality and its
content!), but, of course, with the freedom of
God's grace. Ubi et quanto visum est Deo, not in
themselves but in virtue of divine decision as
expressed from time to time in the Bible and
proclamation."[26] Thus we may and must say that
revelation takes place illic et tunc visum est Deo.
Here we have to speak of not a possibility, but
the reality of the Word of God. Furthermore, it
becomes clear then that the revealed Word of God
is not conditioned but rather it is itself the
condition; it does not, as the written word and
proclaimed word does, signify the twofold concrete
relation in which the Word is spoken to us; revelation is the Word of God itself, the act of its
utterance.

In point of fact, revelatio or apokalypsis
does not differ from the Person of Jesus Christ,
and it does not differ from the reconciliation
which took place in Him. Thus Barth says, "To
say revelation is to say 'The Word became flesh'."[27]
This revelation, furthermore, the Word became flesh,
means that Barth is grounding his assertions within
the Trinity, i.e., by the will of the Father, by

the mission of the Son and by the Holy Spirit. Only
as knowledge of God proceeds from God as free
undeserved grace, can it have any sense or meaning.
Consequently, both Scripture and Church proclamation
renounce any other foundation save that which God
Himself has given once and for all by having spoken.[28]
Indeed, as Barth ultimately concludes this comprehensive section of his Dogmatics, he makes it very
clear that

> It is Jesus Christ Himself who speaks for
> Himself in it [Revelation] , and needs no
> witness save His Holy Spirit and is glad
> of the faith of His own in the promise
> received and grasped. It is this indepen-
> dent and unsurpassable origin for the Word
> of God which comes to us that we mean when
> we speak of its third --- materially we
> should say its first -- form, its form as
> the revealed Word of God.[29]

4. The Unity of the Word of God

In all that we have said it is quite clear that
Barth is not referring to three several words of
God. The Word is one and the same in all its forms,
i.e., Revelation, the Bible and "proclamation"
all mean the same thing. There is no distinction
or degree of value between these three forms. Of
course, as we have noted, the first form, i.e.,
Revelation is the one which established the other
two. But Barth says, "It itself never meets us
anywhere in abstract form, of it precisely our
knowledge is only indirect, arising out of Scripture or in proclamation."[30] He draws up a brief
schedule of mutual relationships which give expression to his thought:

> The revealed Word of God we know only from
> the Scripture adopted by Church proclamation,
> or from Church proclamation based on Scrip-
> ture.

> The written Word of God we know only through
> the revelation which makes proclamation
> possible, or through the proclamation made
> possible by revelation.

The proclaimed Word of God we know only
by knowing the revelation attested through
Scripture, or by knowing the Scripture which
attests revelation.[31]

The relationship between this scheme and Barth's
conception of the Trinity is quite apparent. As
there is a doctrine of the three-in-oneness with
this concept of revelation, there is also the doctrine of the three-in-oneness in God. In substitu-
ting the divine person names for revelation,
Scripture and proclamation, we discover that we
encounter the same mutual relationships, determinations, difficulties and light in the one as in
the other. This we feel shall be evident when we
consider the doctrine of the Trinity as the immediate
implicate of revelation in the succeeding chapter.

B. THE KNOWABILITY OF THE WORD OF GOD

At the outset of his discussion of this section
Barth cautions his readers that the question which
he wants to answer does not concern the actuality
of the cognition of the Word of God, but rather the
nature of this cognition, its acuality, the how of
which remains as hidden as God Himself, being pre-
supposed. Furthermore, he asserts that in this
connection, the concept of cognition must be taken
in a general and indefinite way as to allow for
every correction, limitation, or inversion that the
Word of God may demand.

1. The Word of God and Man.

Barth maintains that the Word of God is an
occurrence that concerns and affects the reality
of man, and admits that logically and factually
there must be a power of cognition on the part of
man corresponding to this occurrence. Thus Barth
writes:

As certainly as the Word of God is primarily
and originally the Word which God speaks by
and to Himself in eternal hiddenness...as
certainly as it is, in revelation, Scripture,

-55-

and preaching, the Word addressed to men,
we cannot speak it, we cannot think of it
without at once remembering also the man
who hears and thereby knows it. The Word
of God, Jesus Christ, as the being of the
Church, faces us irresistibly with the realization that men they were and men they
will be, who are there intended and addressed
and so characterized as the addressees, but
also themselves bearers of the Word.[32]

Or, as he puts it later on in his Evangelical Theology:

The Word of God is the Word that God spoke,
speaks, and will speak in the midst of all
men. Regardless of whether it is heard or
not, it is, in itself, directed to all men.
It is the Word of God's work upon men, for
men and with men. His work is not mute;
rather it speaks with a loud voice....We are
speaking of the God of the Gospel, his work
and his action, and of the Gospel in which
his work and action are at the same time his
speech. This is his Word, the Logos, in
which the theological logia, logic, and
language have their creative basis and life.[33]

These considerations raise, for Barth, the anthropological question, i.e., the capability or non-
capability of man in this respect. While Barth maintains that there must be a power of cognition on
the part of man corresponding to the occurrence,
he denies that it is man's by nature and contends
that in distinction to all other powers of cognition
it becomes as a concomitant of its object. Sebastian
A. Matczak, in his volume Karl Barth on God, points
up this position by indicating that readiness or
capability when applied to the Divinity is an
attitude rooted in His essence, i.e., His wesen
and also in His action (handeln) by which we know
Him. Consequently, the possibility of our knowledge
of God is primarily a function of the readiness
of God Himself. There corresponds, in man, a human
readiness. This correspondence in man, however,
differs in that in man it is not autonomous

(selbstandig), i.e., rooted in man's essence and
action, but is rather rooted in God Himself.[34]
The Word of God would no longer be grace, if such
a power were man's own. Barth articulates the
point in these words: "God's Word ceases to be
grace when we ascribe to man a disposition toward
this Word, a possibility of knowledge independent
of it and peculiar in itself, over against this
Word."[35] The formulae which man uses to describe
the real content of the Word of God are not identical with the content of the Word which God
Himself utters and in which He invariably expresses Himself in the way indicated by the
formulae. What takes place is not that the determining factor resides in man. Rather, it is with
the real content of the real Word of God that the
possibility of knowing corresponding to the real Word
of God has come to man, that it sets forth quite
inconceivable novum in direct contrast to all his
ability and capacity and is to be regarded as a
pure fact, like the Word of God itself. "In other
words, in the real knowledge of the Word of God
in which that beginning alone will be made, there
is also the event that it is possible, that that
being can be made...Men can know the Word of God
because and so far as God wills that they should
know it, because and so far over against the will
of God there is only the weakness of disobedience,
and because so far as there is revelation of the will
of God in His Word, in which the weakness of disobedience is removed."[36] It is clear, therefore,
that the knowledge which man does possess, according
to Barth, is knowledge in abstraction from the
Word of God; it is not a question of how man in
general can know the Word of God, but rather, "it
is the man who really knows the Word of God who
also knows that he can bring no capacity to this
knowledge but must first receive all capacity."[37]
What Barth is doing here is making reference to the
event of the real knowledge of the Word of God, the
force of which lies not in the reference, but
in that to which it refers. The fact of the knowledge of the Word of God does not presuppose its
possibility in man but in coming to man it brings
possibility with it.[38] Here Barth is trying to

sharpen the separation of theology or faith from
any type of philosophy for even philosophy cannot
perform this negative service of indicating the
impossibility of knowing the Word of God apart from
its reality which is its presupposition. Thus the
cogency of all that man says depends upon whether
he is granted the Word of God; it does not at all
depend on oneself, but on the Word of God itself,
since this Word is the living, personal and free God.

2. The Word of God and Experience.

Having defined knowledge as the confirmation
of human acquaintance with an object whereby its
trueness becomes a determining factor in the existence of the man who knows, and that it becomes
possible for man in the event of the reality of the
Word of God, Barth attempts to explain the possibility by means of the concept of experience. Experience of the Word of God always takes place in
an act of human self-determination. However, it is
not as this act that it is experience of the Word of
God. Thus Barth writes, "no determination which
man can give himself is as such determination by
the Word of God."[39] Nor is this experience a
matter of the collaboration of divine and human
determinations, whether Pelagian, Semi-Pelagian
or Augustinian. All these theories are to be
rejected because they are in basic contradiction,
as far as Barth is concerned, to the self-know-
ledge of man found in the real experience of the
Word of God as we know it from the Biblical promise. The content of this Word precludes ascribing
the possibility of experiencing it either wholly
or partially, or equating the divine possibility,
that realizes itself in such experience, dialectically with a human possibility. The being together
on the same level, and their possibility of being
together, cannot be understood. Nor is there any
particular meaning in asserting man's self-
determination, even dialectically, against the
determination of man by God. "For the very reason
that it is self-determination it is subordinate to
determination by God."[40] It needs this determination
by God in order to be experience of His Word.

We understand that, according to Barth, man is not partly or wholly receptive and passive in the experience of God's Word; his self-determination is not negated. Rather the man who really cognizes the Word of God understands himself only as he exists in his activity of self-determination. The Word of God comes as a summons to him, and the Gehor, the response, is either right response or disobedience. Which response it is does not lie within his province. But in either instance man's response or decision is subject to the judgment or determination of God to Whom alone his obedience or disobedience is apparent. Nevertheless, it makes no difference to the fact that it is his hearing, his action, his decision. In a summary argument on this point, Barth states:

> human existence means human self-determination. If in experience of the Word of God the point is the determination of human existence, and so of human self-determination by the Word of God, by self-determination is to be understood the activity of the combined powers, in the activity of which man is man, without fundamental rejection of this or that human possibility. All such emphases or rejections are in this context to be refused on the score of method, because they are the results or presuppositions of a general philosophical anthropology, by the constructions of which we dare not let ourselves be influenced here, whatever right or wrong they may possess on their own ground. Determination of a man's existence by the Word of God when viewed from various sides may equally be well regarded as a determination of feeling, as of will or intellect; psychologically considered in the concrete instance, it may even actually be more the one than the other. But in substance it is definitely a determination of the whole self-determining man.[41]

The existence of God, then, is known through His Revelation and this revelation is His Grace. It is not within the power of man to achieve it; it is not the result of either man's desire or disposition, it is in the hands of God alone. God alone can make it possible for us to deal with revelation and with truth (see, Church Dogmatics, II/1, p. 75). Further, the way to truth cannot even be ascribed to either intuitive or intellectual acts. The grace of God is necessary for the knowledge of God. Although Barth admits that the knowledge of God from revelation, has a human side, this knowledge seen from this perspective is empty and without object, since the object has to be submitted to us by God Himself.

At this point in his argument Barth raises this question: In what does the determination by the Word of God consist? To answer this decisive question Barth articulates the concept of Anerkennung (acknowledgment) and develops it in relation to nine characteristics of the wesen (essence) of the Word of God outlined in The Doctrine of the Word of God: (1) a cognition takes place; (2) a personal relationship; (3) an affirmation of the content of the Word of God; (4) an acknowledgment of the presence of Jesus Christ; (5) a subjection to the Word of God; (6) a decision concerning man, which manifests a qualification of the decision of man for belief or unbelief, for obedience or disobedience; (7) a standing still before a mystery; (8) a being moved by one experience and thought to opposites ones, because God's Word is at one time veiled, at another time unveiled; and, (9) a founding of the whole man on this mystery, lying beyond himself.[42]

In the act of acknowledgment, the life of man, without ceasing to be his self-determining life, has its center, its origin, the meaning of its assumed attitude, outside itself in that which is acknowledged, in dem anerkannten. Thus while it is the doing of man, with reference to the meaning of the assumed attitude, it is not all his doing but a determination which has come to him from that which acknowledged. That which is acknowledged

comes first and then with reference to it and ultimately from it comes acknowledgment. The implication of all this is, as Barth indicates clearly,
"that experience of the Word of God is possible,
but that precisely in view of its meaning and
ground, of its ultimate seriousness and peculiar
content, precisely in view of its truth and
reality it is not experience, it is more than
experience."[43] For Barth this is a formal description of religious experience or consciousness.

One of the problems which arises when considering the possibility of experiencing the Word
of God, and a problem the understanding of which
Barth is anxious to guard against, is whether or
not in the real act of cognizing this Word becomes
man's property, a predicate of his existence,
his possession in the form of an emanation from
the Word or an influxus into man. This Barth
emphatically rejects! Only an acknowledgment
that man does not consummate, and therefore confirm, but that happens to man's sinful and dead
work out of grace, supplies the needed and definite
counterpart to the Word of God. It is, for Barth,
non finitum non capax infiniti, but homo peccator
non capax verbi Domini.[44] Therefore the possibility
of knowing the Word of God is such as can have its
ground and certainty only outside of itself, i.e.,
in the Word of God itself. As Barth puts it: "It
is this real experience of the man claimed by the
Word of God which decides and proves that what
makes it possible lies beyond it."[45]

The certainity of one's affirmation of this
possibility is a certainty of faith. That is to
say, man is not sure of himself, but only of the
Word of God and that not through himself but
through that very Word. It means a turning from
ourselves toward the Word of God and being con-
formed to the Word of God. It is a summons and
an expectation in which the possibility of the
cognition of the Word of God comes to view. By
way of acknowledgment, by way of appeal to grace
already received, and in expectation of new future
grace, he affirms the possibility of knowing the
Word of God.[46]

This involves a tremendous risk; it is an expectation with what Barth calls a trembling assurance and yet an unheard of assurance. He is sure not of himself, but of the Word of God. And, moreover, of the Word of God he is not sure, not of and in himself, but of and in the Word. His assurance is, of course, his assurance, but it has its seat outside of him, in the Word of God, and so it is his assurance by the Word of God being present to him.

> Just because it is in such profound jeopardy, just because it is connected with a sanction which we cannot create but can only hope for, just because it is included in the divine realization and so withdrawn from our reach and so only to be sought there, only to be expected thence, for these reasons and in these ways it is an assurance which bears in itself a metal which makes it superior to any other assurance....[47]

If it is truly assurance of grace already received -- something only God can decide -- then our affirmation of the knowability of the Word of God is a knocking which receives a response.

3. The Word of God and Faith.

This brings us to our final portion in the analysis of the knowability of the Word of God in Karl Barth's overall concept of revelation. And that is a statement of his conception of the Word of God and Faith. Faith is, for him, the miracle of actual cognition of the Word of God and makes this knowledge possible.[48] Concerning this event or occurrence of faith, Barth posits three important points from which flow three qualifications of the conception of the knowability of the Word of God.

(A) Faith is an experience, a concretely fixable, temporal act of a particular person. However, it is true faith only in virtue of the Word, i.e., Christ, "to Whom faith is related, because He gives Himself to it, Who makes faith into faith, into real experience."[49] Thus it is not merely the experience that makes faith to be faith, or the mere acknowledgment

-62-

that makes faith to be faith, but the possibility
arises and consists purely in the Word of God given
to us purely as the object of real knowledge and consequently as the ground of faith itself.

(B) In faith a Gottformigkeit of man takes
place. That is to say, not a deification, but a
conformity and an adaptation of man to the Word.
If this were not the case, either man would no
longer be the subject of faith or faith itself would
cease to exist. There would be no communion between
the speaking God and the hearing man if there were
no analogy of similarity as well as dissimilarity.
In faith, therefore, man is capable in his own
decision of so corresponding with the decision of
God made about him in the Word, that the Word of
God is now heard by him, i.e., he is now the man
addressed by this Word.[50]

This capacity, or ability, which is a capacity
that overtakes the fact that the finitum non capax
infiniti or homo peccator non capax verbi divini,
means that for the man in faith the Word of God is
knowable, that it is spoken to him and that he can
hear it and apprehend it as the Word of God. Furthermore, as this recognition takes place there
is also a togetherness of the Word and man, a oneness of the divine and human logos in faith. This
may be said, not in the form of an analysis of
human consciousness in faith, but in the form of a
postulate directed by the nature of the Word of
God to man's consciousness in faith. Only as we may
and must believe God's Word itself, so too, we
may and must believe our faith in that Word, its
knowability for us, the presence of the forma verbi
amid man's darkness, the presence of Christ in the
darkness of our heart. This possibility, moreover,
is the possibility of a certain and clear knowledge,
not equal to, nor yet unlike the certainity and
clarity in which God knows Himself in His Word.[51]

(C) The final point to be made concerning
Barth's conception of faith is that as a believer
man is wholly dependent upon the object of his
faith. Without in the least denying the fact that
his own experience and action are concerned, that
in faith his is by no means a stone or a block of

marble, but that he is a self-determining being,
that he is by no means submerged in passive
apathetic contemplation, but continues to live
his own thinking, willing, and feeling life; it
must still be affirmed that he cannot regard himself as handelndes Subjekt. "Man acts by believing, but the fact that he believes by acting
is God's act. Man is the subject of faith. It
is not God but man who believes. But the very
fact of a man thus being subject in faith is
bracketed as a predicate of the subject, God,
bracketed exactly as the Creator embraces His
creature, the merciful God sinful man, i.e.,
so that there is no departure from man's being a
subject, and this very thing, the ego of man as
such is still only derivable from the Thou of the
Subject, God."[52] The Word of God becomes knowable by making itself knowable, the possibility
of which is God's miracle in and on us.

This concludes our analysis of Barth's conception of revelation and the knowability of the
Word of God and gives us the background and
foundation necessary for a proper understanding
of his doctrine of the Trinity --- to which we
shall now direct our attention.

CHAPTER 3 NOTES

1. Karl Barth, Church Dogmatics: The Doctrine of the Word of God, Volume I/1 (Edinburgh: T & T Clark, 1960), p. 98.

2. Ibid., (underline added) p. 89.

3. Ibid., p. 51

4. Karl Barth, Church Dogmatics: The Doctrine of the Word of God, Volume I/2 (Edinburgh: T & T Clark, 1960) p. 743.

5. Ibid., p. 90ff.

6. Ibid., pp. 60-67.

7. Karl Barth, "Revelation" in Revelation edited by John Baillie and Hugh Martin (London: Faber & Faber Ltd., 1937), pp. 68-70.

8. Barth, Church Dogmatics, Volume I/1, p. 61.

9. Barth, "Revelation," pp. 68-70.

10. Barth, Church Dogmatics, Volume I/1, p. 99.

11. Ibid., pp. 99-101.

12. Ibid., p. 102.

13. Ibid., p. 104.

14. Ibid., pp. 103-104.

15. Ibid., p. 111.

16. Barth feels that it was in this sense that Augus-understood memoria (in definite connection with the Platonic doctrine of anamnesis) for Augustine writes in his Confessions, Book X, 19, 28: "Unde adest, nisi ex memoria? Nam it cum ab alio commoniti recognoscrimus inde adest. Non enim quasi credimus, sed recordantes approbamus hoc esse quod dictum est. Si autem penitus aboleatur

ex anima, nec admoniti reminiscimur. Neque enim
omni modo adhuc obilite sumus, quod vel iam
oblitos nos esse meminimus." Thus recollection
is finding what is already there, specifically
man's turning inward, his heartsearching and his
homecoming from the outer world to himself, to
find God actually there (Cf. Confessions, Bk. X,
27, 28, 29).

17. Barth, Church Dogmatics, Volume I/1, pp. 114-117.

18. Ibid., p. 121.

19. Ibid., pp. 120-121.

20. Ibid., pp. 123-124; Cf., Barth, "Revelation,"
pp. 67-68.

21. Barth, Church Dogmatics, Volume I/1, p. 124.

22. Ibid., pp. 124-131.

23. Ibid., p. 134.

24. Ibid., p. 129.

25. Barth, "Revelation," p. 53.

26. Barth, Church Dogmatics, Volume I/1, pp. 132-133.

27. Ibid., p. 134.

28. Ibid., p. 135. We have taken care in noting that
while Barth speaks of the Word of God in three
forms: proclaimed in preaching, written in Scripture
and "revealed" in Christ, it is only the last, "the
revelation," that is really the divine Word. In
this connection, although it is not our specific task
to go into great detail in this area, it is nevertheless incumbent upon us to make at least two points,
or rather, to raise two points of inquiry. First:
we may say that in his thought here, and elsewhere,
e.g., in his doctrine of the Church, Karl Barth
is vulnerable to the charge of "occasionalism".
Second: and this is related to the first point, the

written and spoken Word appear rather obscure
and instrumental at best. That is to say, if we
want to meet the Divine Word, we must go back by
way of the written Word and the spoken Word to
the point where the Word became flesh. Thus we
may safely say that the written Word and the spoken
Word are not continuous with the first revelation in the Christ. I think, however, that while
we may admit that these are weaknesses in Barth's
thought at this point, (as Gustav Wingren apparently
does, cf., Theology in Conflict), we may also see
that he is perfectly justified, or that he has a
legitimate fear, at least, in the respect that
the freedom of God in His activity, in His revelation, will be restricted or limited severely. Put
another way, he is justified because he clearly
recognizes the possibility of Scripture and Church
proclamation becoming the self-authenticated Word
rather than having their foundation in the Word of
God itself and rather than becoming the Word of God
by attesting to past revelation and promising
future revelation. Barth tries to clarify this in
his scheme for the unity of the Word. Nevertheless,
it is not in the power of the Bible and/or proclamation to make it true that the Deus dixit
of the Church is present in any one of her given
times or situations. This defense would also be
valid, I believe, for the charge which some make
against his doctrine of the Church.

29. Ibid., p. 135.

30. Ibid., p. 136.

31. Ibid., p. 136.

32. Ibid., p. 218.

33. Karl Barth, Evangelical Theology: An Introduction
(New York: Holt, Rinehart & Winston, 1963), pp. 18-
19.

34. Sebastian Matzcak, Karl Barth on God (New York:
St. Paul Publications, 1963); cf., Barth, Church
Dogmatics, Volume II/1, pp. 70, 72.

35. Barth, Church Dogmatics, Volume I/1, p. 221.

36. Ibid., pp. 223-224. It might be well to note here the way in which Barth analyzes the problem of the Creator-creature relationship. It is evident that his emphasis is upon the situation, i.e., the external and the objective. In this statement, e.g., the weakness of disobedience is almost removed mechanically. The point is also evident in his doctrine of reconciliation, as we shall see later.

37. Ibid., p. 224.

38. In this connection Barth means presupposition in the sense of recollection of the Word of God and the hope of its advent, i.e., an appeal to the Bible Word and expectation of fulfillment.

39. Barth, Church Dogmatics, Volume I/1, p. 227.

40. Ibid., p. 228.

41. Ibid., p. 233.

42. Ibid., pp. 234-238.

43. Ibid., p. 238.

44. Ibid., p. 238.

45. Ibid., p. 252.

46. Ibid., p. 257ff.

47. Ibid., p. 259.

48. Ibid., p. 261.

49. Ibid., p. 263.

50. Ibid., pp. 273-275.

51. Ibid., pp. 278-280.

52. Ibid., p. 281.

CHAPTER IV

THE DOCTRINE OF THE TRINITY

IN THE

THEOLOGY OF KARL BARTH

We have taken a substantial amount of time and
space to articulate, as clearly as possible, how
Karl Barth conceives of revelation. The reason for
this background will now be self-evident for it is
our contention that his doctrine of the Trinity
is an analysis, an interpretation, an implication
of revelation, and, therefore, essentially identical with the content of revelation. The question
that arises is, of course, whether this analysis as
such is a proper interpretation. The doctrine
itself is not contained in Scripture explicitly,
but rather only the root upon which intellectual
reflection and formulation must take place. On
this particular point we might suggest that the
distinctive aspect of Karl Barth's thought is the
way in which he understands this root, so that
for him the doctrine is not a synthesis or reconciliation of several elements, but what may be
called an analytical development of the central
fact of revelation. With this in mind let us proceed with our presentation of Barth's understanding
of the doctrine of the Trinity.

A. THE PLACE OF THE DOCTRINE OF THE TRINITY

The great significance of the Trinity is
immediately self-evident in the fact that Karl
Barth places this doctrine at the beginning of
his dogmatics, not merely as the first doctrine or
at the beginning of the doctrine of God, but in the
prolegomena to his Church Dogmatics. In placing
the doctrine of the Trinity at the head of his
dogmatics he is adopting a position which, in view
of the history of dogmatic theology, is quite
isolated. Nevertheless, although this position is
not frequently found, it is not absolutely unique,
for Peter Lombard in his Sentences and St. Bonventure
in his Breviloquium, likewise, took this posture.[1]
Furthermore, and even more importantly, the understanding of the doctrine of the Trinity, which is
delineated here in this prolegomena, is a continually
recurring motif throughout his Dogmatics. The
Trinity, in this way, is not seen as an isolated
affirmation about God, but is fundamental to all
aspects of the Christian faith. For example, the
relation of the Father and Son are seen as the type

-71-

of all Creator-creature relations or of all inter-
creaturely relations. Or in the doctrine of God
proper, the tri-unity of God is the basis, the
inner truth of His self-disclosure as Lord; it is
as Triune that God is in Himself living and loving.[2]

While this motif is found recurring elsewhere,
our main purpose is to consider now its formulation
and expression in the Doctrine of the Word of God,
i.e., in the prolegomena. In this work Karl Barth
explicitly states the primary reason for placing
the Trinity at the head of dogmatics and in the
prolegomena. This is absolutely necessary for
as soon as we ask the question, "To whom and what,
etc., do the Scriptures attest?" i.e., as soon as
we inquire into revelation, we discover that a
unique question is involved:

> It absolutely insists upon being regarded
> in its uniqueness. That means, it absolutely
> insists upon being regarded from the side of
> its Subject, God. It is the revelation of
> Him who is called Yahweh in the Old Testament
> and theos or concretely kyrios in the New
> Testament.[3]

This necessarily involves not only Who is the self-
revealing God, but also How this happens and What
is the result or effect upon the man whom it befalls.
These questions are individual and independent and
yet inseparable. Therefore, by the statement: "God
reveals Himself," we are to understand that it is
God who reveals Himself, that He reveals Himself
through Himself and that He reveals Himself. The
answers to these questions are identical. Barth says,
"If we wish really to regard the revelation from the
side of its Subject, God, then above all we must
realize that this Subject, God, the Revealer, is
identical with His act in revelation, identical
also with its effect."[4]

Here Barth is not merely making a rationalistic
deduction from the general proposition that God
reveals Himself, but rather he is summarizing what
revelation means by the use of a formula.[5] The

testimony is at one and the same time testimony
to Him Who is the Revealer and to What is achieved
in the Revelation. "Thus it is God Himself, it
is the same God in unimpaired unity, Who according
to the Bible's understanding of revelation is the
revealing God, and the event of revelation, and
its effect upon man."[6] There is no attempt in
the Bible, nor does Barth believe that it is possible,
to dissolve this unity and make it uniformity by
removing the boundaries which separate the three
forms of His being God in revelation. It is
rather, by consideration of this unimpaired
"unity and variety of God in His revelation
attested Scripture...(that) we are confronted with
the problem of the doctrine of the Trinity."[7]

We have already noted that Barth deviates
from the history of dogmatics by placing the doctrine
of the Trinity ahead of Holy Scripture (or, as in
Roman Catholic dogmatics, of the authority of the
Church) as the principium cognoscendi. Barth justifies his position by saying: "it is difficult to
see how in regard to Holy Scripture we can tell
what is significant for the holiness of this very
Scripture, unless previously it has been made
clear --- naturally from Holy Scripture itself ---
Who that God is Whose revelation makes Scripture
Holy."[8] Similarly, and particularly with reference
to both Catholic and Protestant dogmatics --- old
and new --- Barth feels that the questions of the
existence of God and the nature of God cannot be
determined except on the basis of the decisive
question, Who God is. The answer given to the
question is in the doctrine of the Trinity and
since it is, it is quite proper to place this
doctrine at the head of dogmatics. Here Barth
appeals to John Calvin, a man, who, according to
Karl Barth, did not follow his own principle:

> For how can the human mind, which has not
> yet been able to ascertain what the body
> of the sun consists, though it is daily
> presented to the eye, bring down the
> boundless essence of God to its little
> measure? Nay, how can it, under its own

guidance, penetrate to a knowledge of the
substance of God? ...Wherefore let us
willingly leave to God the knowledge of
himself. In the words of Hilary, "He alone
is a fit witness to himself who is known
only by himself." This knowledge then if
we would leave to God, we must conceive of
him as he has made himself known, and in
our inquiries make application to no other
quarter than his word.[9]

Furthermore, Barth sees the doctrine of the
Trinity as a safeguard against getting totally
lost in vague and useless considerations and coming
to totally irrelevant conclusions. That is, by
becoming involved in such considerations, as How
do we know God? Does God exist? What is God and then,
only finally and ultimately, Who is our God? In
following this procedure we are brought to conclusions that may prove contradictory and embarrassing,
conclusions that must be dealt with first and
foremost when dealing with the doctrine of the
Trinity (see especially pp. 346-348). It is the
doctrine of the Trinity then which is the fundamental distinction of the Christian doctrine of God
as Christian in the face of all other possibilities
of the doctrine of God or concepts of revelation.
There is an interdependence of revelation and
the Trinity and any doctrine, therefore, that
purports to be revelation must be considered
in trinitarian terms. In other words, the question
to which the doctrine of the Trinity is an answer
is the question of the reality of revelation. When
the question is asked, "Who is the self-revealing
God? the Bible answers us in such a way that we are
impelled to consider the Three-in-Oneness of God.
Moreover, the other two questions, what God does,
and what He effects are, as we say, primarily
answered by new answers to the first question, Who
is He? The problem of these three, like and yet
different, different and yet like, answers to these
questions is the problem of the doctrine of the
Trinity. The problem of revelation stands or falls
primarily with this problem."[10]

What has been articulated here by Barth has
not received the voice of approval in all quarters.
Hardly!! First, for example, Emil Brunner, in his
Dogmatik, criticized Barth on several points.
He states that Barth assigns an importance to the
doctrine of the Trinity which does not legitimately
belong to it, but only to the revelation itself.
That is: it is said that he (Barth) does not distinguish between the problem of the Trinity which
is set by the message of the Bible and the doctrine
of the Trinity. Brunner feels that Barth does not
make the doctrine a product of reflection, but
rather, that he makes it to be the kergyma itself.[11]
The reason for this, in the mind of Brunner, is that
Barth is very fearful of any possibility of a
natural theology.

It is apparent, furthermore, that these two
theologians differed over the function of the prolegomena in a dogmatic theology. For while Brunner
saw the need for the prolegomena merely to state
formal theological principles, Barth saw the need
also for a substantive treatment of the doctrine
of the Trinity. By making the Trinity the content
of the prolegomena, Karl Barth is also calling
attention to the all pervasive importance and influence of this doctrine.

Concerning the question of the equation of
doctrine and kerygma, I cannot help but feel that
this was an error, or a misunderstanding, on the
part of Brunner. While Barth does emphasize the
revelational basis of the doctrine, i.e., the root,
he does not equate revelation and doctrine. Karl
Barth says quite explicitly: "The statement or
statements about the Trinity of God cannot claim
to be directly identical with the statement about
revelation or with the revelation itself."[12] What
Barth does rather is to develop the conception of
the immanent or essential Trinity from the eccnomic
or relational Trinity, thus using revelation as
a means of avoiding a purely speculative apprcach,[13]
of which, as Brunner rightly stated, he is apprehen-
sive.

-75-

Brunner claims that the Trinity is not a Biblical doctrine. However, neither does Barth believe or claim it to be a Biblical doctrine in the sense that as such it is to be found in Scripture (in fact, Barth states that no dogma, which is by definition -- reflection --, is to be found there in that sense). He declares the doctrine to be an analysis, an interpretation and an intellectual formulation only indirectly identical with the revelation. The doctrine of the Trinity is an analysis of revelation, i.e., what it designates.

Barth maintains that an investigation of the unity and diversity between the ways in which God reveals Himself brings us "up against the problem of the Trinity."[14] Or he can say that the Biblical witness to revelation is the "root" or "ground" of the doctrine of the Trinity.[15]

In contradistinction to Schleiermacher, who relegated the doctrine of the Trinity to the end of his Dogmatics because it was speculative and did not represent an immediate implication of the Christian's self-consciousness, and in opposition to most of his followers who regarded it as a speculative doctrine that was peripheral in Christian theology, Barth intends that it is the doctrine of the Trinity which fundamentally distinguishes the Christian doctrine of God as Christian --- it is it, therefore which also marks off the Christian concept of revelation as Christian, in face of all other possibilities of God and concepts of revelation.[16]

Barth, then wishes to indicate the primacy of the doctrine of the Trinity and does so by manifesting its tie, though indirect, with revelation, which is the root of this theological doctrine. Let us then proceed to our next consideration which is this ground or root of the doctrine of the Trinity, i.e., revelation.

B. THE ROOT OF THE DOCTRINE OF THE TRINITY

According to Karl Barth, the revelation attested

by Scripture means at least two things: first, it means that God Himself addresses man as "thou", and is therefore present Himself in His speaking. It is God Who speaks; God Who unveils; God Who addresses. Therefore, Barth maintains: "Revelation in Dei loquantis persona."[17] This revelation is not something less than God Himself, something which we get behind and examine on the basis of a higher and more profound knowledge of God. We may speak, of course, of the many different consequences and implications that this revelation may bring, but God Himself is the content of revelation (and the form as well). Revelation has being in itself because it is God Himself addressing man. As Barth says:

> ...Scripture and proclamation may be the Word of God. They must become it (revelation). Revelation must not first become it. In it reposes and lives the fulness of the original being of the Word of God, Existent in itself.[18]

Second: God's revelation is a revelation of His Godhead, i.e., His coming to man as Lord. God in His revelation as Lord brings Himself before another as a superior will, as an I before a thou.

The statement: "God reveals Himself as Lord" is specifically designated by Barth as the root or ground of the doctrine of the Trinity. Initially two points must be made. First: the statements about the Trinity of God cannot be, or even claim to be, directly identical with the revelation itself. Rather the doctrine is an analysis of the statement God reveals Himself, i.e., what it designates. The text of this doctrine is throughout connected with the Biblical witness to revelation, but it also includes, in its interpretation and exposition, certain other concepts. These are additional reflections necessary to explain what is present and is also the reason why Barth designates revelation merely the root of the doctrine of the Trinity.[19] It is necessary as a work of the Church, as that which is at all times the task of

dogma and dogmatics, to struggle against error and
to struggle for the relevancy of proclamation. Thus
in addition to its Biblical root, the doctrine trans-
lates and expounds upon it availing itself of
other data than those contained in the text --- con-
fronting what is there in the text also with something new in order to explain what is there.

This has always been the case and Barth points
out that the Fathers of the Early Church, the leaders
of the Councils, indeed, even the Reformers themselves were quite aware that the doctrine of the
Trinity is not in the Bible. But he also points
out, "they rightly denied that for legitimacy,
i.e., 'Biblicity' of the Church dogma and of a
church theology it was a matter of ipsa etiam verba
(i.e., the Word of Holy Scripture) totidem syllabis
et liberis exprimere (M. Chemnit, Loci, ed. 1591
I p. 34). That would mean an inquia lex for the
Church, a condemnation of all Scripture exposition
which really consisted of explicare quod Scriptura
testatum consignatumque est (Calvin, Instit. I, 13,
3)."20

Second: by so describing revelation, Barth
asserts that propositions about the Trinity may be
indirectly identical with propositions about revelation, since these propositions would be both
analytical and interpretative. Barth strongly
asserts that the doctrine is a theoretical formulation which is a necessary and relevant analysis of
revelation. The point here is that the doctrine
is derived from analysis of the one central fact to
which the Bible bears witness -- the act of God in
revelation --- that is, therefore, indirectly
identical with this witness to revelation. Thus
Barth rests the doctrine of the Trinity not merely
upon Biblical trinitarian indications, nor is
he piecing together affirmations of Christ's deity
and the deity of the Holy Spirit and their unity with
the Father, but on that which unites the whole of
the Biblical witness.21

Barth analyzes the statement "God reveals Himself" in terms of three concepts: Revealer, Revelation,

and Revealedness. All of these concepts do not,
however, have the same weight. Similarly, in the
doctrine of the Trinity all three concepts:
Father, Son and Holy Spirit do not have the same
weight. In the former it is the second, "God's
action in His revelation -- revelation in answer
to the question What God does, and thus the predicate of the sentence -- which is the real theme
of the biblical witness."[22] In the latter the
chief emphasis has been on God the Son. However,
in substance, all three have equal weight and
the first and third concepts come to expression as
necessary counterparts of the second. Let us then
proceed to briefly examine each of these concepts.
(1) Revelation is first God's self-unveiling, His
becoming a Thou to men, His existing for them as
God, His coming to them in Christ. This means
that God assumes a form. It is something which
man cannot supply himself, but only that which God
can give him and actually does give him in His
revelation. Barth maintains here that this is not
impossible or incongrous, nor does it involve subordination. It is "not something that goes without
saying but an event."[23] It is a move on God's
part making manifest His Lordship which consists
in His freedom to be God the Son, to be God for us.
This fact of revelation declares that it is His
property to distinguish Himself from Himself,
i.e., in Himself to be, hiddenly, God and yet at
the same time to be God in quite a different way,
namely, manifestly, i.e. God a second time. Thus
we may see that for Barth the Lordship of God is
seen in this Sonship, i.e., in God's freedom to
be the Son, to be Himself and yet to be other than
Himself at the same time.[24] Here we see a utiliza-
tion of Sören Kierkegaard's Incarnation of the
Absolute Paradox, as Robert Franks suggests.[25]

        (2) Further analysis of the statement "God
reveals Himself" indicates that "Revelation in
the Bible means the self-unveiling, imparted to
men, of the God Who according to His nature cannot
be unveiled to man."[26] There are several important
points to be made with respect to this observation.
First: we may see that in His revelation God is

both the Revelation and the Revealer. It is as
Deus revelatus, and as Deus revelatus only, that
we may have any word to say about the Deus
absconditus. Barth states: "there is no way and
no bridge, of whom we could not say or have to
say one single word, had He not of His own initiative met us as Deus Revelatus."[27] Second: God is
free to reveal or not to reveal. He is not contained by the form of Revelation but rather speaks
through it and remains free in it for the form
itself does not reveal, speak, comfort, work or
help but only God in it (see also Church Dogmatics
I/1 § 4, (2) (3), pp. 111-135). It is His freedom,
His decision to be present. Third and finally
we see again a paradox for God is ever and again
a mystery; He is inscrutable and does not belong
to the realm of the creaturely knowledge of God.
He is veiled and yet unveiled; He assumes a form
and is also free to give Himself afresh or refuse
to give Himself; He is God a second time and yet
remains equal within Himself. Here Barth makes
reference to the rather remarkable circumstances
of revelation in Exodus 3 wherein we have in the
midst of the revelation the refusal of a name
(Exodus 3:13-15). God reveals Himself -- but it
is always God Who is revealing Himself -- when, as
and how He wishes.

     (3) Finally, the statement that "God reveals
Himself" as the Lord means that the self-unveiling
is imparted to men. Previous inquiry was made
about the source of revelation. Now the question
is asked: Where does it go? This revelation,
Barth declares, takes place not only in man's
sphere, but reaches man himself. It is concrete
revelation to concrete men. It is an historical
event, not in the ordinary sense of a single event
narrated in the Biblical account, i.e., as appre-
hensible by a neutral observer, but rather in the
sense of a concrete event between God and man. It
is a unique narrative that took place more or
less exactly determined. This event, which is
to a large extent obscure, is open to historical
criticism. Nevertheless, Barth declares:

     ...that makes no difference to the fact that

-80-

by the thing it calls revelation the Bible
always means a unique event, one occurring
in that place and at that time....an event
that took place there and only there, then
and only then, between God and men. The
divine self-unveiling of which it (the
Bible) tells, together with the holiness it
ascribes to this act of His, is imparted not
simply to man, but to such and such men
(emphasis Barth's) in a perfectly definite
situation.28

Thus there is a third sense in which God is Lord in
His revelation, i.e., in His freedom to "become the
God of such and such men" concretely, i.e., in a
concrete situation, in an event. This is what
Barth means by an historical revealedness, His becoming truly a THOU to men. Moreover, this is
God's revealedness, His being imparted to men
so that in their experience and concepts they are
able to respond to Him. Without this, revelation
would not be revelation. It is God in His revealedness, His effect upon man, i.e., the effective
meeting between God and man. In this Barth sees
confirmation of the statement that God reveals
Himself as Lord. In this third sense God reveals
Himself as Spirit, as the Spirit of the Father and
of the Son, and at the same time as the one God,
but now this time as the same one God in this
particular way.29

        In summary then the statement about the revela-
tion is an attempt to garner the whole witness of
Scripture to the encounter of God with man. It
indicates that in this encounter, there is both
unity and variety. It calls attention to the
three elements of unveiling, veiling and impartation, of form, freedom and historicity, or, of the
Son, the Father and the Spirit. These three elements do not need to be added to each other or
reconciled with one another, for they are clearly
and totally inseparable and interdependent. Barth
says in closing this discussion: "We have established no more than this, that the Biblical revelation is implicitly, and in some places explicitly,
also an indication of the doctrine of the Trinity.

-81-

In its ground-plan it must be interpreted as the
ground-plan also of the doctrine of the Trinity."[30]
It is because Barth understands the root of the
doctrine of the Trinity in this way that he is
able to speak of the doctrine itself as an analysis
of revelation and as indirectly identical with
statements about revelation.

Cyril Richardson, Professor of Church History at
Union Theological Seminary in New York, agrees that
Karl Barth has done more than any other modern
theologian to restore the doctrine of the Trinity
to a place of first rank in Christian theology,
but also finds Karl Barth's treatment of the
Trinity open to several criticisms and objections.
First: as in the Logos doctrine of the great era of
the Patristics, Richardson argues that the distinction within the Godhead implies that God is more
God in the first term, the first mode, then He is
in the second. Second: he states that it is to
deny the quality of the absolute to attempt to
relate his beyondness and his relatedness. Any
such attempt is doomed to failure, he declares,
by the very nature of the terms. Richardson
states: "If the one is in any sense begotten of
the other, then the other is no longer absolute.
The result of deriving God in his visible and
encountered nature from God in his invisibility and
self-sufficiency is to compromise the latter...
we can say no more than that we hold both these
things to be true...He is God in these two ways
of which neither is prior, neither is primary."[31]
Furthermore, Richardson declares that Barth does
not carry this basic distinction back into his
concept of God as Father. That is: here logic
should have drived Barth to deal primarily with
God as completely hidden. But, says, Richardson,
Barth invokes the doctrine of appropriations, and
treats God under the category of "Creator" which
is really to abandon the basic declaration, or
distinction, of veiled and unveiled and to relate
the Father so closely to the creation that He
loses the absolute character implied in His being
truly "unveiled."[32]

Against the first charge of Richardson's Barth
declares (not directly to Richardson) that it consists in the freedom of God Himself to distinguish
Himself from Himself, to become other than Himself,
"and yet remain as He was."[33] Furthermore, Barth
argues that God, because of His absolute freedom,
can become

> so unlike Himself that He is God in such a
> way as not to be bound to His secret eter-
> nity and eternal secrecy, but also can and
> will and really does assume a temporal form ---
> this ability, desire and real action of God
> we might now regard as a first confirmation
> of our sentence, God reveals Himself as
> Lord.[34]

Barth's position seems very clear: if God is God
and man is man, who is to declare that He cannot
do this? Why not? Further, the root or ground of
the analysis here presented is revelation, i.e., God's
self-unveiling. To say that God cannot posit
Himself over against Himself would be to place
improper restrictions upon His Divine Essence and
His Divine freedom. In addition to this, herein
lies the theme of all community-ness. The God who
meets man is none other than the God who already
meets Himself and his community as Father, Son
and Holy Spirit. He wills community for man, not
because of need, but because He has community in
His trinitarian structure. This community-ness
is beautifully and almost poetically expressed
by Barth in his consideration of the Holy Spirit;
thus he writes:

> And God is Love, Love goes forth out from
> Him as His Love, as the Spirit which He
> Himself is, because He posits Himself as
> the Father and so posits Himself as the Son.
> In the Son of His Love, i.e., in the Son
> in and with whom He brings Himself forth
> as Love, He then brings forth also in the
> opus ad extra; in creation the creaturely re-
> ality distinct from Himself and in revelation
> reconciliation and peace for the creature

-83-

that has fallen away from Him. The Love
which meets us in reconciliation and looking backwards from that, in creation, is
therefore and thereby Love, the highest
law and the ultimate reality, because God
is Love, antecedently in Himself; not
merely a principle of the connection of
separation and communion, but Love which
wills and affirms, seeks and finds in
separation the other thing, the Other
Person in communion also, in order to will
and to affirm, to seek and to find communion with it (Him) in separation also.
Because God is Love antecedently in
Himself, therefore, love exists and holds
good as the reality of God in the work of
revelation and in the work of creation.
But He is Love antecedently in Himself,
by positing Himself as the Father of the
Son.[35]

This analysis is valid for to say that God would be
other than He reveals Himself to be, i.e., different
antecedently in Himself than He is in His economic
relations would be, in effect, to deny revelation.[36]

Regarding the use of the doctrine of appropriations, one must realize that it is a mere
appropriation and as such does not include the truth
of perichoresis, the intercommunity of the Father
and the Son and the Spirit in their essence and
operation.[37] To make such appropriations may be
a derivative and improper procedure, since, in
actuality, it is not only the Father, but God as
Father, Son, and Holy Spirit Who is our Creator
and Reconciler and Redeemer: God is one and undivided
in His operation as in His essence. To that
extent we may agree with Richardson, but so, too,
does Barth. Nevertheless, the doctrine of appropriations may be used and the distinctions made may
be beneficial and what is said true as well, i.e.,
that the Father is the Creator. It is improper,
however, in the sense that it is one-sided, but
the knowledge of God based upon it is true, though
relative knowledge. It conveys truth by pointing
to the

affinity between the order of God's three
modes of existence on the one hand, and that
of the three sides of His operation as
Creator, Reconcilier, and Redeemer on the
other. Between the relation of the Father
to the Son and the relation of the Creator
to the creature there exists once for all
an affinity....In view of this affinity
it is not only allowed but enjoined upon us,
to ascribe as a proprium to God the Father
in particular, and to regard the Father
peculariter, precisely as the Creator.38

This revelation puts us in touch with the Father,
the Revealer from Whom are all things and with the
Holy Spirit Whose work it is to open men's lives
to receive Jesus the Christ as grace and truth.
There is no contradiction here since it is all
God's work and the Holy Spirit does not add a
new completedness to an laready finished work, but
only "completes" revelation by making it known to
us and real in us. This, of course, is stated
quite adequately by Barth when he points to Jesus
Christ as the objective reality of revelation;39
and the Holy Spirit as the subjective reality.40
Since revelation is all of God and since it is the
Triune God Who is made known, one must so speak
of revelation in its objective and subjective
elements. Nor should this necessarily be thought
of as taking away man's choice or his faith or his
freedom; it is rather, for Barth, the power of all
three.

     Moreover, these distinctions in the operations
(Creator, Reconciler, and Redeemer) are only distinctions within the sphere of human conceivability.
The concepts: Father, Son and Holy Spirit (or
Revealer, Revelation, and Revealedness) are only
analogous to the eternal inconceivable distinctions.
None of the concepts which we use can be adequate;
they are only be useful in pointing beyond themselves
to the problem posed by Scripture and the eternal
nature of God. We must take care in pointing them
to the problem posed by Scripture and the eternal
nature of God. We must take care in again pointing

out that God's hiddenness is not something which
stands behind His trinitarian nature, so that He
might be something other than Triune, other than
as He reveals Himself.

C. VESTIGIUM TRINITATIS

Karl Barth rejects all other "roots" of the
doctrine of the Trinity and asserts, as we have
just previously argued, that the genuine root is
ONLY in revelation. "The doctrine of the Trinity
is nothing else than the unfolding of the knowledge
that Jesus is the Christ or the Lord. By saying
that from this root proceeds the doctrine of the
Trinity, we are saying in a spirit of polemical
criticism that it can proceed from nowhere else."[41]

Under this heading, Barth includes all the
various analogues of the Trinity which have been
discovered in creaturely existence, as presumably
showing a similarity to, or being a copy of, the
Triune nature of God. Some of these analogues
have been found in culture, history, religion,
psychology, and nature. However, all are to be
held suspect, since they are posited as traces of
the trinitarian God in creaturely existence, and
as such, apart from revelation, they leave the
possibility open for a "second root" of the
doctrine of the Trinity. This would then raise
the additional question: which of the two
contiguous roots would be primary and which secondary?
But this raises two additional questions: is the
derivation of the doctrine from the Biblical revelation merely a confirmation of the revelation in
creation? And, is this then, reducing theology
to anthropology or cosmology?[42]

Barth recognizes that the original function of
the analogies was not to this purpose, but to find
language for expression, to show how the Trinity
is capable of self-expression in created things.
Nevertheless, he is fearful that, in the ambiguity
that arises when various vestigia are taken
seriously, the doorway to analogia entis is left
wide open. Barth's apprehension concerning various

-86-

vestigia is significant. He firmly believed the
assertion of the possibility of these _vestigia_
trinitatis is not only important for the root of the
doctrine of the Trinity itself, but for the question of revelation generally, for the question of
basing theology solely on revelation and for the
distinctiveness of theology itself. As he states
in an excursus, "the question is whether these
vestigia trinitatis do not, by the conclusions
which result from recognizing them...compel us to
pass over first to that cheery double tract of
'revelation' and 'prime revelation' (Paul Althaus),
and then from this half-measure ... to genuine
Roman Catholic theology of the _analogia entis_."[43]
Barth also argues, in a later writing, that certainly we can make use of science and philosophy,
but then only if they have been very carefully
sterilized."[44] When we speak of God and when we
speak of Incarnation it is Barth's contention that
we are dealing with a novel event which has no
counterpart in these areas of study. Moreover,
the _analogia entis_, the doctrine which holds that
reason reflects on the universe and seeks to
deduce the existence of God because a certain likeness is perceived between the final being of creation
and the supreme being of which the latter was the
utmost cause. But for Barth there is no being
common to God and man,[45] so that we can reason from
one to the other. If such knowledge ever existed,
it could not, furthermore, have given us what we
receive in special revelation, i.e., that God is
Triune,[46] or God as Revealer.[47] In Barth's opinion,
it is at this point that Roman Catholicism has
tried to establish a knowledge of the Creation apart
from the fact that He is Reconciler and Redeemer.
This has led to a separation between the being of
God and the act of God. After discussing all of
the analogies Barth asks: "What are we to say to all
this material, what are we to do with it.?"[48]
He concludes that it is not to be overvalued nor
applied as a foundation or root, but rather that it
is at its very best supplementary, a non-obligatory
illustration of the Creed. In support of his
position he draws upon some very significant
allies: Irenaeus of Lyons,[49] Augustine of Hippo,[50]
Peter Lombard,[51] and St. Thomas Aquinas himself.[52]

Further, in passing from interpretation, which
Barth defines as saying the same thing in different
terms, to illustrations, which he defines as,
saying the same thing in different terms, something
other than revelation always sets itself at the
center calling attention to itself. Thus he feels
that revelation will properly submit to interpretation but not to illustration. He closes by
stating that there is naturally one vestigium
trinitatis in creatura that is real: He manifestly
creates Himself a vestigium of Himself and so of
His three-in-oneness.[53]

We may quite agree with Barth that we must
reject any attempt to root the doctrine of the
Trinity in any illustration. However, we may also
raise several questions of our own regarding this
treatment. Is it necessary that we must forsake
all attempts to illustrate the concept of the
Trinity providing that we recognize and understand
the appropriateness and usefulness of the illustration? It is also difficult, even though Barth
lays different emphases in definition, to see a
real qualitative difference between interpretation
and illustration. In this regard there is a
particularly valid objection. That is: Barth
recognizes the necessity of analogy and indeed
that it plays an important role in understanding
the subjectivity of God, i.e., by analogy with
human subjectivity. If this is the case, then
why not with the divine variety or the divine
three-in-oneness. Of course, we may surely say
that no analogy is really adequate, i.e., is not
intrinsically satisfactory as an analogy for the
divine tri-unity. Nevertheless, this is no reason
to cease from using analogy as an aid to the communication of the divine truth.[54]

D. THE DIVINE UNITY AND VARIETY

Karl Barth treats this subject under the section
"God's Three-in-Oneness." This doctrine, as rightly
built up in the Church as correctly interpreting
Biblical revelation, regarding the Subject of this
revelation, is, for Barth, a decisive confirmation

into the insight that God is one. The faith of this
formula is not a faith with three objects for three
objects of faith would mean three gods. But the
so-called "Three Persons" in God are never three
Gods.[55]

(1) There is then a oneness in the threeness
of God. Further, the Lordship of God, of which
Barth has been speaking and to which we have
referred, is in the language of the ancient Church
the essence of God, the deitas or divinitas, the
divine ousia or essentia. The unity of this essence,
Barth asserts, is not removed by the threeness
of the "Persons" but it is in the threeness of the
"persons" that its unity consists. That is:

...three-in-oneness does not mean a threefold deity, either in the sense of a plurality
of deities or in the sense of a plurality of
individuals or parts within the one deity....
The name of Father, Son, and Spirit means
that God is the one God in a threefold repetition; and that in such a way, that this
repetition itself is grounded in His Godhead;
....in this repetition He is the one God.[56]

In other words, God meets us, according to the Scripture as One Thou in threefold repetition, therefore,
unquestionably as one person. Here also Barth calls
upon the Franciscan Bonaventura for support:
"Quidquid est in Deo, est ipse Deus unus et solus;"
whatever may have to be said about the distinction
in God, it can never be said or mean a distinction
of the divine being and existence (essentia et esse).[57]

Barth, of course, recognizes the difficulty that
arises with the modern concept of the term "person."
He notes that there belongs to the one single
essence, i.e., the Lordship of God, which is not to
be tripled by the doctrine of the Trinity, and to
that essence only, what we call "personality."
Person, says Barth, "has nothing to do directly
with personality. Thus the meaning of the doctrine
of the Trinity is not that there are three personali-
ties. ....We are speaking not of the three divine
'I's' but thrice of the one divine I. The concept

-89-

of the equality of essence (ὁμοουσία, consubstantia) in Father, Son, and Spirit is thus at every point and pre-eminently to be regarded in the sense of identity of essence. From the identity follows the equality of essence in the "Persons'."[58] This concept of personality is important in preventing the Divine Thou from being made into an it. Neither can this ever mean three thous or three its if we hold to the unity of the Lordship of Christ with the Lordship of the Father. For on that unity rests the claim for the equality of essence of the Son with the Father. This concept of ὁμοουσία, co-equality of essence in Father, Son and Spirit is to be regarded in the sense of identity of essence and from this identity follows the equality of essence in the persons.[59]

It is quite evident that these are to be considered not as opposing interests, artificially brought into agreement; rather, in dealing with this problem of oneness and threeness, of threeness and oneness, we are dealing with revelation where the two are one. If we take this revelation seriously, as the presence of God, then in no sense can Christ and the Spirit be subordinate hypostases. In predicate and object in the concept of revelation we must be dealing over and again with the Subject.[60] That is: Revelation and Revealedness must be equal to the Revealer or, put another way, the Producer must be equal to His Product which is Himself in distinction.[61]

(2) The concern for the unity of the Godhead is not to be considered as meaning that the distinctions in the divine activity are unimportant. On the contrary, the threeness which we observe may and should call attention to, and indicate the problem of, the eternal threeness of God. These distinctions, however, are not such as would involve the distinction or division of the divine essence of God. We are permitted to recognize that in revelation God meets us "in constantly different action, always in one of His modes of existence, or better put, distinguished or characterized from time to time by one or another of His modes of

existence."[62] However, this does not enable us to
apportion the types of action ontologically among
the Father, Son, and Holy Spirit, as if we were
able to grasp the eternal distinction by their
operational manifestations. God is one in His
operation -- opera trinitatis ad extra indivisa sunt
-- and our distinctions are made only within the
sphere of our conceptions. If we try to do more
than this, then we either make God into three Gods
(Tri-theism) or we make Him at one time Creator,
at another Reconciler, etc., (Sabellianism) as
if these activities were separable.

Thus Barth feels that God's freedom rests on
His inconceivability, but he states:

> it is...legitimate for us, on the basis of a
> revelation which takes place within the
> sphere and within the limits of human con-
> ceivability [here we may see the principle --
> fides quarens intellectum --- clearly in
> operation] to distinguish the three modes of
> existence of the one God....The limit of our
> conception lies in the fact that in conceiving
> these distinctions we do not conceive the
> distinctions in the divine modes of existence.[63]

In other words, even though these distinctions,
manifesting the three-in-oneness of God in His
operation, really take place in the sphere and limits
of human conceivability, they do not primarily signify
the last word in the hidden essence of God. The
only way we may speak of the eternal distinctions
is analogically. Thus, as we have indicated before,
the doctrine of appropriations is invoked.

(3) To go beyond the three-in-oneness and the
one-in-threeness is an impossibility, even though,
Barth declares, these formulae are unsatisfactory
and one-sided. Inevitably, in each conception,
there is an emphasis of the one at the expense of
the other. It is at this point that the conception
of the three-in-oneness comes into prominence.
However, this is nothing more than a confirmation
of the two. This conflation produces an advantage

which can never be more than a dialectical union
and distinction of the mutual relation of these two
unsatisfactory formulae. This dialectic of unity
and Trinity finds its completion in the concept of
perichoresis or circumincessio.

[It] signifies at once the confirmation
of the distinction between the modes of
existence (none of them would be what it
is -- not even the Father! -- apart
from its coexistence with the others) and
the relativisation of it (none of them
exists as a special individual, all three
'in-exist' in one another, they exist only
in common as modes of the existence of the
one God and Lord who posits Himself from
eternity to eternity).[64]

This concept of the definite and complete participation by each mode in the other modes of existence
flows from the understanding that the one essence
of God is truly and indivisibly present in His
existence as Father, Son and Spirit. This does
not mean that the modes of existence are identical
with each other, but that they are co-present in
each other, just as the knowledge of the Father
is not identical with the knowledge of the Son,
but the Father is knowable only in the Son. In
this way also, Barth disavows all attempts to
regard Father, Son and Spirit as distinctions
in the content of the divine activity or as attributes or departments of the divine essence and
activity. This insistence by Barth is found in
the rule for theologizing on the Trinity, opera
trinitatis ad extra indivisa sunt.[65] The acceptance of this rule follows from his conception
of the unity of God's essence and of the perichoresis.

What Barth is insisting upon is that God is
as much Creator and Redeemer in His mode of existence as Son as He is Reconciler. God is known
as Creator and Redeemer only when He is known
as Reconciler. The Lordship of God is the same in
Creation, Reconciliation, and Redemption. The

-92-

manner in which we perceive this, from the limits
of our own human conceptual ability, while important and indispensable, can only serve to indicate
a threeness in God's eternal being: a repetitic
aeternitatis in aeternitate.

E. INTERNAL RELATIONS

At this point we shall briefly discuss Barth's
understanding of the distinction between God as
Creator, God as Reconciler, and God as Redeemer,
i.e., Father, Son, and Holy Spirit. It will be re-
called that Barth arrived at these distinctions
per appropriationem. We have seen that the ground
of the divine threefoldness is found in the distinctions of "form" or of "relationship" which are
implicit in the revelation occurrence, e.g., when
we raise the question Who is God? we immediately discover that three questions are involved (see above
p. 43ff.). We have also seen this exemplified in
the concepts: Revealer, Revelation and Revealedness;
Creator, Reconciler and Redeemer, and most especially,
Father Son and Holy Spirit.

Barth grounds the original relations, and consequently the distinction of the divine modes,
upon the whole pattern or order which is involved
in the revelation as attested in the New Testament.
This is pre-eminently signified by the terms just
referred to: Father, Son and Holy Spirit. In so
doing Barth is not basing his conception of relations
on the sort of scriptural literalism which thinks
that references to the begottenness of the Son and
the breathing or proceeding of the Holy Spirit can
be taken as unquestionable deliverances about the
internal life of the trinitarian persons. Nor are
the relations of origins or processions here conceived of as a part of a rationalistic or quasi-
rationalistic deduction of the doctrine of the
Trinity such as we find in St. Anselm.[66] Rather,
Barth, who consistently desires to speak of God as
He is antecedently in Himself from the standpoint
of revelation, grounds the original relations on a
broader base. As expressed earlier, it is necessary
that we make the doctrine of the immanent Trinity
conform exactly to the economic Trinity in content.[67]

In other words, he is seeking to base affirmations regarding the internal relations precisely upon the divine oikonomia, the arrangement of the elements of the revelation to which the scriptures bear witness.

In accord with the previous statement of the conformity of the immanent Trinity to the economic Trinity, we may indicate the relations by which the various modes of existence are distinct from one another. God as Father is God in that mode of existence in which He is the originator, i.e., He is the ground or presupposition of the Son and the Holy Spirit; He is the principle from Whom the Son and the Spirit proceed.[68] In speaking of procession, however, Barth sees it in a distinctive way qualifying the traditional concept of communicatio essentiae for he feels that if the essence of the Son is from the Father and the Spirit is from the Father and the Son, strictly speaking, it denies the unity of the essence of God. Even the concept of communicatio essentiae, if taken strictly, actually asserts something which cannot be said without denying the unity of the essence of God.[69] The procession of the second "person" can only mean the existence of the one essence of God in a second way, i.e., God positing Himself. By this Barth means that in this self-positing God is Father of Jesus Christ and Jesus Christ is Son of the Father. Indeed he asserts that "this most powerful figure then can and is meant merely to summon us to knowledge so as never to keep us tied to it alone, rather to lead our view at once onwards beyond itself to the Object."[70] It is not, properly speaking, the modes of existence which subsist, but God Who subsists in three modes of existence. Thus Barth speaks frequently of the "intradivine relations" in terms of movement or repetitio aeternitatis in aeternitate.

It follows from what has been said that when Barth speaks of the generation of the Son or the "procession" of the Word, he is using fragile and inadequate figures. Nevertheless, they are indispensable and complementary.

The figure of the Father and Son,... is not

the only one by which we have to make clear to
ourselves the concept of the divinity of Christ.
Alongside of it in the New Testament itself
and in the language of the Church there stands
the other one, that Jesus Christ is the Word
of God. According to this figure He is, as
a second mode of God's existence distinct from
the first mode, and once more essentially
at one with it, just as the Word which someone
speaks is a thing distinct from himself, and
yet as his word essentially no whit different
from himself. We say the same thing, whether
we say the "Son of God" or the "Word of God"
--- verbum suum qui est Filius eius (Irenaeus
C. a. h. II, 30, 9).[71]

Here Barth also calls upon St. Thomas Aquinas when he
declares: "Jesus Christ is God's eternal emanati
intelligibilis upote verbi intelligibilis a dicente
quod manet in ipso."[72] From these observations
Barth concludes that "the first figure is nearer
the mark, when we regard the action of God in Jesus
Christ materially as reconciliation, the second nearer
the mark, when we look at the action formally as
revelation."[73] Each of these figures, however, only
points to an object for which it is inadequate. It
would not be advisable, in Barth's judgment, to
bring the concept of the divinity of Christ right
down to the same denominator as the metaphor "Word."

As the terms Son and Word only point to, and
indicate, the second mode of existence in which God
distinguishes Himself from Himself, the figure of
the Father and Son and the words generatio and
processio only call attention to the inconceivable
relation between God in His mode of being as Father
and God in His mode of being as Son. These figures
indicate that the kind of relationship, i.e., the
kind of variety and continuity that exists
finitely between father and son or speaker and word,
the kind of existence of the first for the second
and the kind of existence of the second for the
first, "that kind of twoness and oneness in the same
existence" is the kind of relationship or

existence in which "He becomes manifest to us in Jesus Christ, and the other one from which He is He who is manifest in Jesus Christ."[74] Thus Barth is able to speak of the mutual love of Father and Son. Here we are at once reminded that these figures only summon us to acknowledge by their figurativeness. For we do not exactly know what we say, when we call God Father and Son, and what we say, we say in such a way that in our speech and in our thoughts it is an untruth; the truth we express is hidden and un- searchable. However, in thus naming God, neither figure can give us the nature, the "how" of the production from God in God, but each can point to the "thatness" and simply suggest a way that has analogical validity.

These aspects or elements of our knowledge of the generation or procession of the Son also applies to the procession of the Holy Spirit. The distinction in revelation is one in which "in the one revelation the Son or Word represents the human element of God being assigned to man, the Spirit the element of God being appropriated by man."[75] Thus there is an eternal distinction in reality between what the Son and what the Spirit are antecedently in themselves.

Directly involved with this concept of "inner relations" based upon the pattern or order of revelation, i.e., the conformity of the immanent Trinity with the economic Trinity, is the filioque controversy. In Karl Barth contemporary theology finds a powerful defender of this concept of the double procession. His points may be summarized as follows:

(1) There must be an actual conformity between God as He reveals Himself and as He is antecedently in Himself. Thus if the Spirit Who operates upon us externally is the Spirit of the Father and the Son, He can be none other in the internal relations of the immanent Trinity.

(2) The filioque expresses the communion between the Father and the Son without which the communion

of God and man would lack warranty. That is: if this communion did not exist antecedently, and there would be no room for it if the Spirit proceeded from the Father alone, the communion of the Spirit between God and man would lack a foundation. As Barth puts it: "the special feature of the Holy Spirit's divine mode of existence consists, paradoxically enough, in Him being the common factor between the mode of existence of God the Father and that of God the Son. Not what is common to them, so far as they are one God, but what is common to them so far as they are the Father and the Son."[76]

(3) If we deny the _filioque_ the door might be left open for a corresponding interpretation of revelation, which may produce a distorted view of the mission of the Spirit as being separate and distinct from the mission of the Son.[77] That is: Barth rejects the phrase "through the Son" as a substitute for "and the Son" on the ground that the former "does not lead to the thought of a complete consubstantial communion between Father and Son as the essence of the Spirit."[78] The consequence of this denial of the _filioque_ is the fear that Christ may be by-passed. That is to say, the relationship between God and man may then be viewed as purely a Creator-creature relationship, thus assuming a naturalistic and unethical character.

The way in which Barth conceives of the Holy Spirit as the communion of the Father and the Son (point 2 above) deserves further comment because of its great importance to him, although it is not always perfectly clear. In approaching the subject Barth points out that _pneuma_ is neuter and that in the Niceno-Constantinopolitan Creed the term _kyrios_ is used adjectivally of the Spirit. Therefore, this calls attention to the special feature of the Spirit's divine mode of existence, which is, paradoxically, that He is "the common factor between the mode of existence of God the Father and that of God the Son. Not what is common to them, so far as they are one God, but what is common to them so far as they are the Father and the Son."[79]

There are several questions which may reasonably be raised concerning this treatment. First: assuming that Barth's presuppositions and analyses are valid, it is difficult to understand the co-equality of the hypostases in the manner in which he presents it, for he seems to attribute more to the third mode of existence, i.e., the Spirit, in that this mode is held to be the unifying bond within the Godhead, than he does of the other two hypostases. Would it not then be more natural to identify the Spirit with ousia of God rather than with hypostasis (this seems to be implied in the text of note 76)? Or is it even possible for one hypostasis to unite the two remaining hypostases? Furthermore, if this is the case, and if Barth is correct, we then seem to have an ontological priority of the Spirit over the Father and the Son entailing a relative subordinationism of the Father and the Son.

Clarification of this matter of communityness or communion of the Father and the Son is attempted by stating that Barth's affirmation could be better reconstructed from the fact that God in His revelation is, as Spirit, communion, impartation, love or gift. Thus we should be moving directly from the understanding of the Spirit in revelation as communion and love to the eternal basis of that love in the communion of the Father and the Son. Barth does come close to this position when he asserts that the filioque is the expression of the knowledge of the communion between the Father and the Son and that this knowledge is nothing else than the knowledge of the ground and confirmation of the communion between God and man, as a divine eternal truth as created in revelation by the Holy Spirit. The significance of this concept of the intradivine two-sided communion is not only that God is present to man, but that man is also present to God. This is possible because the God Who meets man is already the God Who meets Himself and has community as Father, Son, and Holy Spirit; the God Who wills community because He has community in His trinitarian structure; not because He needs fellowship but because He loves, i.e., a love of self-giving and not a love of need.[80]

On the other hand, would it not be equally plausible to state that there is no real need (except for his demanding conformity of the immanent Trinity with the economic Trinity) for a binding together of the Godhead? For if each of the three modes of existence participate in each other, if each "inexist" in each other (as he also maintains), and in the divine ousia, is it necessary then for them to be bound by the Spirit into that in which they already exist? This seems to be merely an arbitrary distinction necessitated by a previous commitment to conformity in every detail.

Finally, the question may be raised whether those who defend the double procession of the Spirit ought not be consistent and maintain the double procession of the son, that is

> since the Creed explicitly maintains the office of the Holy Spirit in connection with the external mission of the Son ("was incarnate from the Holy Spirit"), there would seem to be even stronger ground for the interpolation of a Spirituque "begotten of his Father before all worlds."81

With this analysis of the doctrines of internal relations we conclude this portion of our presentation of Karl Barth's consideration of the doctrine of the Trinity. In the immediately succeeding chapter we shall attempt to point out, albeit briefly, what we feel are his most significant contributions to theology on this particular issue.

CHAPTER 4 NOTES

1. Karl Barth, Church Dogmatics, Volume I/1,
"The Doctrine of the Word of God," translated
by C. F. Thomson (Edinburgh: T & T Clark, 1960),
p. 345.

2. Ibid., p. 451.

3. Ibid., p. 339.

4. Ibid., p. 340.

5. In observing this we see the connection to the
Anselmic formula fides quarens intellectum. This
indicates the relation or correspondence between the
doctrine of the Trinity on the one hand and revelation as the root on the other.

6. Barth, op. cit., p. 343, Cf. p. 344.

7. Ibid., p. 344.

8. Ibid., p. 345.

9. John Calvin, Institutes of the Christian Religion (translated by Henry Beveridge, Volume I
(Grand Rapids: Wm. B. Eerdmans Publishing Company,
1957), Book I, 13, (21), p. 128. Quoted by Karl
Barth in the Church Dogmatics, Volume I/1, p. 345.

10. Barth, op. cit., p. 348; Cf., p. 436.

11. Emil Brunner, The Christian Doctrine of God
(Philadelphia: The Westminster Press, 1950),
pp. 235ff.

12. Barth, op. cit., pp. 353-354. While Brunner
does not articulate his doctrine of the Trinity in
the prolegomena of his Dogmatik, he really does
not differ from Barth in any substantive manner.
It is true that his formal presentation of the
"high" theological doctrine does not appear until
his Chapter 16, i.e., after his presentation of
the "Nature of God and His Divine attributes."
Yet, when he treats, in Chapter 1, the subject of
the "Name of God" and makes such statements as

"God is only known where He Himself makes His
Name known....Apart from this self-manifestation
He is unknowable...." (p. 120.), he is in essence
agreeing with Professor Karl Barth.

13. Barth's endeavor to avoid the construction of
a philosophical system or being tied to any system
is clearly in evidence in his treatment of the
knowability of the Word of God. He appeals to
the event of revelation which he conceives of as
being wholly unrelated to philosophy or general
human experience and which, in fact, would lose
its revelational character and import the moment
such a relation occurred.

14. Barth, op. cit., p. 348ff.

15. Ibid., pp. 349-383 (we shall return to this
point very shortly).

16. Ibid., p. 396.

17. Ibid., p. 349.

18. Ibid., p. 351.

19. Ibid., pp. 352-354.

20. Ibid., p. 354.

21. This was noted in a previous section on the
Trinity as the basic problem in theology, i.e.,
the self-revelation of God in Christ.

22. Barth, Church Dogmatics, Volume I/1, pp. 361-
362; Cf., Robert Franks, The Doctrine of the Trinity
(Gerald Duckworth & Co., Ltd., 1953), pp. 176-184.

23. Ibid., p. 363. This event does not mean that
God in His second mode of being is less God than in
His first mode of being, i.e., His hidden mode of
being. Here He is just different, i.e., God in a
way that He can be God for us. Although there is
three-in-One and distinction, there is also
community, a complete perichoresis. That is to say,

none of the modes of existence would be what they
are apart from their co-existence with the others,
nor do they exist separately but all three "in-
exist" in one another. We shall come to this point
in our discussion shortly (See Church Dogmatics,
Volume I/1, pp. 472-473 for confirmation).

24. Ibid., p. 368.

25. Franks, Op. Cit., p. 179.

26. Barth, Church Dogmatics, Volume I/1, p. 368.

27. Ibid.

28. Ibid., pp. 374-375.

29. Ibid., p. 381.

30. Ibid., pp. 382-383.

31. Cyril C. Richardson, The Doctrine of the Trinity
(New York: Abingdon Press, 1958), pp. 58-59, 67.
While Professor Cyril Richardson is critical of the
classical patterns of trinitarian thinking as being
contradictory, he himself champions a view which is
itself a basic contradiction in thought, i.e., as
Absolute and Related.

32. Ibid., pp. 67-68.

33. Barth, op. cit., p. 367.

34. Ibid.

35. Ibid., p. 553.

36. This denial is tantamount to modalism. The doctrine of the Trinity asserts that God is God only
as Father, Son and Holy Spirit, i.e., that the three
"moments" or "elements" of His self-revelation are
not foreign to His being as God. In opposition to
modalism, therefore, it affirms that God Who reveals
Himself can be our God because His revelation, His
willingness to be our God, "is grounded and typified
in His own essence, in His Godness itself," Barth,

op. cit., p. 440. (See also pp. 438-439.)

37. Ibid., p. 455.

38. Ibid.

39. Karl Barth, Church Dogmatics, Volume I/2, "The Doctrine of the Word of God," (Edinburgh: T & T Clark, 1960), pp. 1-25.

40. Ibid., pp. 203-242.

41. Ibid., p. 384.

42. Ibid., pp. 384-385.

43. Ibid., p. 385.

44. Karl Barth, Evangelical Theology: An Introduction (New York: Holt, Reinhart & Winston, 1963), p. 109.

45. Karl Barth, Church Dogmatics, Volume II/1, "The Doctrine of God" (Edinburgh: T & T Clark, 1957), p. 243.

46. Ibid., pp. 79ff.

47. Karl Barth, Church Dogmatics, Volume IV/1, "The Doctrine of Reconciliation" (Edinburgh: T & T Clark, 1956), p. 81.

48. Barth, Church Dogmatics, Volume I/1, p. 389.

49. Irenaeus of Lyons, Against Heresies, 2, 5, 1.

50. Augustine of Hippo, Confessions, Book XIII, 11.

51. Peter Lombard, Sentences I dist. 3f.

52. St. Thomas Aquinas, Summa Theologica I, Qu. 32, art. 1.

53. Barth, Church Dogmatics, Volume I/1, pp. 396, 398-399.

54. This does not preclude the use of all analogy for Barth himself employs the analogia relationis and analogia fidei.

55. Barth, Church Dogmatics, Volume I/1, p. 400.

56. Ibid., p. 402.

57. St. Bonaventura, Breviloquium I, 4, as quoted by Barth Church Dogmatics, Volume I/1, p. 389.

58. Barth, Church Dogmatics, Volume I/1, p. 402.

59. Ibid., pp. 501-503.

60. This position of Barth's is not always consistent. E.g., on page 416 he states that the divine modes are distinguished without inequality in their essence or decrease in their activity, but are, however, inequal in their original relations. How can God be unequal to Himself even in distinction?

61. Barth, Church Dogmatics, I/1, pp. 404-406; Cf., pp. 414-416.

62. Ibid., p. 416.

63. Ibid., p. 427.

64. Ibid., p. 425. This doctrine of co-inherence or perichoresis or circumincession is a classical formulation which really involves the identity of the divine ousia as expressed in each Person. We find it expressed classically, for example, in Athanasius, in the Cappadocians and in the 'super-Athanasian', Cyril of Alexandria. The term perichoresis, which has been attributed to pseudo-Cyril in the area of trinitarian theology, was previously employed in Christology. Cf., G. L. Prestige, God in Patristic Thought (London: William Heinemann Ltd., 1936), pp. 260-265; 282-300.

65. Ibid., p. 430. This rule is found substantively is St. Augustine: "Sicut inseparabilis sunt, ita inseparabiliter operantur." (De Trinitate I,4).

66. Anselm, Monologium (LaSalle: Open Court Publishing Co., 1962), translated by S. W. Deane, Chapters 29ff.

67. See above pp. 92ff. and pp. 111ff.

68. This is, at least formally, the traditional doctrine of the principium or source according to which the Father is the principle from Whom the Son and the Spirit proceed. Cf., G. L. Prestige, op. cit., pp. 249, 260-265.

69. Barth, Church Dogmatics, Volume I/1, p. 494.

70. Ibid.

71. Ibid., p. 497.

72. St. Thomas Aquinas, S. T. I, qu. 27. art. 1 as quoted by Karl Barth in Church Dogmatics, Volume I/1, p. 497.

73. Ibid., p. 497; Cf., pp. 499, 500.

74. Ibid., p. 494.

75. Ibid., p. 542.

76. Ibid., p. 537.

77. George S. Hendry, The Holy Spirit in Christian Theology, (Philadelphia: The Westminster Press, 1956), p. 43f.

78. Barth, op. cit., p. 551.

79. Ibid., p. 537.

80. Ibid., p. 551. There still is an ontological priority of the Spirit over the Father and the Son causing a relative subordination of the Father (and the Son).

81. Hendry, op. cit., p. 44.

CHAPTER V

THE SIGNIFICANCE OF KARL BARTH'S

DOCTRINE OF THE TRINITY

Since we have already presented a detailed analysis of Karl Barth's concept of revelation and the doctrine of the Trinity as the immediate implicate of that revelation, we are now in a position to attempt to point up, or single out, some of the significant contributions which the thought of Karl Barth has made in this very difficult area of trinitarian theology. In the succeeding chapters, we shall proceed further with an analysis and evaluation of his thought by attempting to see how it has made its impact on other selected areas of his theological reflection, since we have consistently maintained that the concepts of revelation and the Trinity are central and are continually recurring motifs. Let us now turn to the task at hand.

It is the doctrine of the Trinity which fundamentally distinguishes the Christian doctrine of God as Christian --- it is it, therefore, also, which makes or marks off the Christian concept of revelation as Christian, in face of all other possible doctrines of God and in face of all other possible concepts of revelation.[1]

First: we have seen the primary importance of this doctrine of the Trinity by its strategic location and explication in the prolegomena of the Church Dogmatics. The reason for this location is not that it is merely an artificial or arbitrary assignment, but rather, that it calls attention to the all-pervasive influence of the Trinity for the Christian faith and because it is considered to be the immediate implicate or the immediate interpretation of revelation which is its root. It is, therefore, an explication of the unity and variety of God in His revelation, an analysis which is content is "indirectly" identical with the revelation described in the New Testament.

When we consider the actual structure of, and elaboration of, the doctrine as such, we find it to be in essential agreement with the classical and Catholic doctrines.[2] Furthermore, Barth is not alone in his repudiation of the social analogy of the

Trinity. But what is distinctive about Barth's
position is the new light given to the classical
views, i.e., the conception of the single basis
of the doctrine based on revelation. Thus, as we
have stated, the doctrine of the Trinity is seen to
arise as an implication or interpretation of the
whole witness of the Scripture. It is then a
witness to both the divine unity and the distinctions
of relationship which are implicit and explicit in
the event of revelation. It is not a synthesis;
it is not a harmonization of various affirmations
of faith, but it is an analysis which is "indirectly" identical with the content of revelation.
It is from this understanding that Barth is able to
make intelligible the classical claim for centrality
of this concept of God and to manifest its all-
pervasive importance.

Second: Barth's method of reaching back from
the economic Trinity to the "internal or original
relations," avoids the objections which are usually
directed at the Thomistic scheme with its elaboration of analogy from intellectual or volitional
processes. Further, the economy of revelation
makes it equally possible to speak of the internal
relations (we have raised some questions here,
previously), i.e., Revelation presupposes a
Revealer, Reconciliation a Creator, the Son a Father,
for this pattern is as much a part of the revelation
and salvation to which the New Testament bears witness as is the distinctiveness of Revealer and
Revelation, Father and Son, Creator and Redeemer.

Third: Barth's trinitarianism has been indicated in the form of a polemic; that is, the
difficulty that arises in the concepts of natural
and special revelation. We noted in the section
Vestigium Trinitatis of Chapter IV that Karl Barth
rejects all other roots of the doctrine of the
Trinity and declares that the Trinity is rooted
solely in revelation. The question is asked, then,
if the knowledge of God which is expressed in the
doctrine of the Trinity stands in opposition to
all other knowledge of God. The response to this
question may be in the negative, in that, while
Barth argues that the knowledge of the Father, Son,

and Holy Spirit is rooted entirely in the revelation
to which the Scriptures bear witness, this does
not itself exclude the possibility of an apprehension
or revelation which is other than, but not discontinuous with, the trinitarian conception. This does
not make, or intend to make, the doctrine of the
Trinity dependent upon the affirmations of a natural
theology or general revelation, for the Trinity
springs directly from the self-disclosure of God
in Christ. Rather, those aspects confirm, enrich,
etc., the monotheism of an analogia entis.3 Barth
is quite emphatic, however, that such a view,
which he strongly rejects, even though guarded,
leaves the door open for a "second root" of the
doctrine. We have seen in this comprehensive
treatise that the great significance of Barth's
trinitarianism is in revelation alone and although
he humbly acknowledges that he has not spoken the
last word, it is doubtful that he would ever have
compromised the very distinct and definite position
he maintained on this point.4

CHAPTER 5 NOTES

1. Karl Barth, Church Dogmatics, Volume I/1 (Edinburgh: T & T Clark, 1960), p. 346.

2. We would also point out that in the Church Dogmatics, Volume I/2, where Barth first articulates his specific Christological position, he is in deep sympathy with the Classical or Primitive formulations, which accounts for his predisposition towards an incarnational emphasis. However, he does, in Volumes IV, 1 and 2 reinterpret his Christology in a novel way using the Reformation concept of the doctrine of the two "states."

3. While Barth is correct in insisting that the Christian conception of the unity of God is not measured by any sort of monotheism, he has not really distinguished properly between "confirming" a sort of monotheism and being "measured by a sort of monotheism."

4. Karl Barth is adamant on this point. Nevertheless, while it may be that he has done a great service for theology in this massive work, it seems that if we were to strictly hold to Barth's position and never make room for any other possibilities, i.e., no revelation other than the trinitarian conception, we would then be placing a severe restriction upon the divine freedom. Consequently, we would hold to the position of the single root of the doctrine with the possibility, the very real possibility, of a revelation which is other than, but not discontinuous with, the trinitarian conception.

CHAPTER VI

AN ANALYSIS OF KARL BARTH'S CHRISTOLOGY

IN VOLUME I/2

A. THE PROBLEM OF CHRISTOLOGY

In a very strict and proper sense Karl Barth
maintains that the reality of revelation, i.e.,
God's self-unveiling, is the Easter story and the
Easter message. Of course, from the Easter story
the Passion of Jesus Christ is inseparable. In it
takes place the hidden work of Jesus Christ which
is subsequently revealed and believed in His
resurrection. Further, to this Passion story
belongs the whole life of Jesus prior to it. Thus
what happens in the entire life and passion of
Jesus Christ is the content of the revelation which
takes place in the event of Easter.1

It becomes necessary, therefore, for us to
inquire into the presuppositions of this event,
hidden in the life and Passion of Christ and revealed in His resurrection. For example, we may
ask: What is the power of this event? How can
it be the Word of Reconciliation, spoken by God
to men, at once divinely true and humanly real
and effective. Further, who is the subject of it?
Who is this Jesus Christ? Earlier, in a previous
section of this work, Barth has already given
answer to these questions, and that most emphatically,
by stating that Jesus Christ is vere Deus vere homo
(section 13). However, since everything depends
upon this standpoint, this position claims special
investigation and consideration for itself.2 As a
whole, that is, in the basic statements of a church
dogmatic, Christology must be dominant and percep-
tible and that is the reason for an express, precise
doctrine of the Person of Jesus Christ.

In discussing the problem of Christology,
"the first essential to a complete grasp of this
matter is a statement about the content of the
incarnation, about God and man becoming one (the
so-called 'two-natures') in Jesus Christ, in which
the mystery of revelation must be brought to its
definite expression."3 Barth puts it in the form
of a crucial statement that constitutes his thesis
for this section, i.e., "that the Eternal Word of
God, chose, sanctified and assumed human nature and

-115-

existence into oneness with Himself, in order thus
as very God and very man, to become the Word of
Reconciliation spoken by God to man."[4] This
statement signifies the mystery of the revelation
of God in Jesus Christ which is the problem of
Christology. That is: this statement describes the
absolute sole point in which the New Testament
witness originates and therefore the absolute
sole point from which a congruous doctrine of
revelation can originate. This is, according to
Barth, our starting-point; we do not seek a higher
vantage point from which we may derive meaning for
this statement. That is to say, we cannot, whether
it be by means of a higher discernment or by
means of a higher authority, get behind this
statement; we can only describe it as our starting point. If we take seriously the fact of
revelation, as the revelation of God, it is not
just an emphatic expression for a discovery man
has made in himself in a Feuerbachian sense;[5]
rather it is a position of absolute necessity.

On the other hand, in dealing with the question Who is Jesus Christ? we must be quite clear
that we are dealing with an ultimate mystery which
"can be contemplated, acknowledged and confessed
as such, but it cannot be solved or transformed
into a non-mystery."[6] Christology must consider
and state who Jesus Christ is, who, in revelation,
exercises God's power over man. But in all cases
Christology's goals and limitations are and must be
determined by the unique object in question, i.e.,
Jesus Christ. However, this must be done in
such a way so that man does not, in effect, exercise a power over God or become the manipulator
of the diety. Thus, Barth says, "This is the place
of Christology. It _faces_ the mystery. _It does not_
stand within the mystery. It can and must not do
more than this. _But it can_ and _must do this._"[7]

Christology is obviously of supreme importance,
most especially for Karl Barth, for the statement
that "Jesus Chris is very God and very man is the
assumption upon which all further reflection must
proceed."[8] This reflection deals with the revelation

-116-

of God as a mystery, being aware that it is such and
acknowledging it as such. But Christology and all
Christological thinking must also "assume its position at the place where the curtain of the Old
Testament is drawn back and the presence of the Son
of God in the flesh is visible and is seen as an
event; yet visible and seen as the event in which
in the midst of time, in the simple datable happening of the existence of Jesus, a 'man like we are',
God the Lord directly and once for all acting Subject. At this point He was Man: God without reserve
and man without reserve."[9] This is the place of
Christology and its question: Who is Jesus Christ?
It is a place that cannot fail to see the mystery;
it is a place where we cannot transmite it into
something which is devoid of mystery. But rather,
it must be treated as it is by its nature as a
mystery. The only other alternative to this
problem of Christology is to drop the question
entirely and, according to Barth, <u>this</u> <u>is</u> <u>exactly</u>
<u>what</u> <u>modern</u> <u>theology</u> <u>(Christology)</u> <u>has</u> <u>done</u>.
Therefore, he sides, at the outset and in principle,
with the Primitive Christological formulation which,
in his opinion, "say the mystery, and on the whole,
was able to preserve it, whatever other faults
it may have been guilty of in detail. All its
efforts were directed towards preserving the mystery."[10] That is, unlike modern Christology,
Primitive Christology did not avoid the problem,
but came to terms with it.

B. <u>VERE</u> <u>DEUS</u>, <u>VERE</u> <u>HOMO</u>

     This statement, <u>vere</u> <u>Deus</u>, <u>vere</u> <u>homo</u>, is
understood to be the correct answer to the question:
Who is Jesus Christ? Furthermore, it is understood by Barth to be the description of the central
New Testament statement, John 1:14, "The Word was
made flesh."[11]

     Early in <u>Volume I/2</u> Barth makes several preli-
minary statements concerning any inquiry into the
dogma of Christology. He writes that in regard to
the exegetical question, it must be noted that
this twofold statement does not very often appear

in so many words in the New Testament. Generally, only one of its two parts appears at certain solemn climaxes in the New Testament witness, where it is clearly the business of the writer to gather up what has been said before coming to the name of Jesus Christ itself.[12] However, this confession does not seem to come very easily from their lips. Thus, as we have seen previously with the doctrine of the Trinity, the Christological dogma also is not to be found as such in the text, but is found in the interpretation or in the commentary on the text.

In regard to the substance of this matter, i.e., the Christological dogma, we may say that the statements about the divinity and the humanity of Jesus Christ which are given in the New Testament, are secondary to the name of Jesus Christ itself. Thus, however central the importance of this matter, Barth maintains that the incarnation should not be considered as the proper content of the New Testament. Rather he declares that the "content of the New Testament is solely the name of Jesus Christ, which, of course, also and above all involves the truth of His Godmanhood. Quite by itself this name signifies the objective reality of revelation. Even the truth of the God-manhood of Christ can do no more than point to this name, and so to the truth of revelation, though it does that indirectly, even when it is directly expressed."[13] In other words, Barth is pointing to the mystery of the revelation of God in Jesus Christ. This has very definite affinities to the way that Barth has given expression to the doctrine of the Trinity for the Christological doctrine or confession is also an interpretation or an analysis of the primary fact of revelation, i.e., Jesus Christ.[14]

As we explore this matter further, we see Barth pointing out that the Christological confession is twofold, i.e, that God's Son is called Jesus of Nazareth and that Jesus of Nazareth is called God's Son. This immediately indicates that the name of Jesus Christ is really the primary fact and that the Christological dogma or confession is

but secondary for it can only point to this name
and the reality which this name denotes. In it
the one original light is refracted, and although
it bears witness to that light, it makes no
statements about it. Only the name Jesus Christ
can bear witness to it as such. Barth himself
raises what is perhaps the most obvious question:
"Does this name not already point to a twofold
statement?"[15] Two observations may be made:
(1) either we have then to discontinue all our
thinking in this area or else (2) we have to adopt
the refracted light in the words and thoughts of
the New Testament, i.e., the Christological confession. We are then faced with the problem
that either God's Son or Word is identical with a
man, with this man, Jesus of Nazareth, or in the
knowledge that a man, this man, Jesus of Nazareth,
is identical with the Son or Word of God. If we
emphasize one of these aspects at the expense of
the other we conclude a Christology that is either
docetic on the one hand or Ebionite on the other.
This has been a central problem in the history
of this doctrine whenever it has been considered
seriously. Nevertheless, "that God's Son or
Word is the man Jesus of Nazareth is the one
Christological thesis of the New Testament; that
the man Jesus of Nazareth is God's Son or Word is
the other."[16] But there is no synthesis of the two.
This does not mean, however, that there is no
place where these two theses are not two but one.
On the contrary, it is the Barthian thesis that
precisely in the reality of revelation, i.e.,
precisely in naming Jesus Christ, the final, ultimate
word has been named, a word that is not a higher
thesis or a further synthesis, but just a name. As
we consider Barth's treatment of Christology, we
shall of necessity be aware that in dealing with
the formulations of very God and very man, we
shall be listening to the two penultimate words that
point to the content of the New Testament, namely,
the name Jesus Christ. In Barth's own words:

> What we hear about the name Jesus Christ
> is witness about God's Son Who became a
> man, about the man who was God's Son, one

related to the other, but not in such a
way that the first ceases to be the first
or the second to be the second, nor in such
a way that the first and second dissolve
into a higher third. Our task is to hear
the first in the second, and therefore, in
a process of thinking and not in a system,
to hear the one in both.[17]

With this in mind let us proceed to analyze Barth's
presentation and consideration of the classical
formulation vere Deus, vere homo.

This statement, vere Deus, vere homo, is considered to be the answer to the question, Who is
Jesus Christ? and Barth understands this answer as
a description of the central New Testament statement
ὁ λόγος σὰρξ ἐγένετο. He therefore uses this
verse (John 1:14) as a guide in discussing the dogmatic statement that Jesus Christ is very God and
very man. We shall proceed along the lines he has
established and discuss briefly the (1) Word made
flesh, (2) the Word made flesh and (3) the Word made
flesh.

1. The Word made flesh.

This Word spoken of in John 1:14 is the divine,
creative, reconciling, redeeming Word which participates without restriction in the divine nature and
existence, the eternal Son of God. It is He Who
proclaims God, Who is invisible for all others, because He alone can proclaim Him, because He is
Himself the only-begotten, in the bosom of the Father,
His Father. It is for this reason that the Word,
and therefore Jesus Christ Who is identified with
the Word, according to John 1:1-18, is "very God."
We must especially note that it is not the deity as
such that was made flesh, for deity does not exist
in itself but only the modes of existence of the
Father, the Son, and the Holy Spirit. But as He
meets us in the Son, He was made flesh in the entire
fullness of deity, which is also that of Father and
Son, for there is a complete perichoresis, a
full circumincessio. Thus at once we made contact
with the mystery of revelation, which is the real

Object of Christology.[18]

Barth's concern for the human situation is
quite evident as he analyzes and reflects upon the
central statement: The Word became flesh. In this
statement "the Word is Subject. Nothing befalls
Him; but in the becoming asserted of Him He acts."[19]
Nevertheless, although this activity took place
and the Word was made flesh, there is no condition
of the world or man which can form the basis of a
claim whereby this becoming could have been predicted.
Even without creation God is not in isolation for
God is in relation to Himself in the eternal modes
of His existence. Therefore, this act is the
freedom of God. It does not belong to any evolutionary process nor is it brought into connection with
creation. For how could Christ ever become possible
as a product of an immanent world evolution? On
the contrary, the Word's becoming flesh is not a
movement of the creature's own. It is a sovereign
divine act; it must be regarded as a new creation,
i.e., the creation of a new man. This arises from
the notion that this act is an act of Lordship
different from creation, i.e., a new act, a new
creation.[20] Two points may be made here: (1) on a
positive note Barth seems, quite clearly, to be
following the Pauline theology expressed cogently
in II Corinthians 5:17-19:

ὥστε εἴ τις ἐν χριστῷ καινὴ κτίσις· τὰ
ἀρχαῖα παρῆλθεν, ἰδοὺ γέγονεν καινά, τὰ
δὲ πάντα ἐκ τοῦ Θεοῦ καταλλάξαντος ἡμᾶς
ἑαυτῷ διὰ χριστοῦ καὶ δόντος ἡμῖν τὴν διακονίαν
τῆς καταλλαγῆς ὡς ὅτι Θεὸς ἦν ἐν χριστῷ
κόσμον αὐτοῖς, τὰ παραπτώματα αὐτῶν· καὶ
θέμενος ἐν ἡμῖν τὸν λόγον τῆς καταλλαγης·

and (2) negatively he raises a polemic against Schleiermacher, who sees Christ, not as the radical
answer of the sovereign God to the gravity of sin,
but rather as the completion or continuation of human

-121-

nature and God-consciousness. For Barth, Schleiermacher did not see the communion between God and his creation as being seriously impaired by human sin. However, if we see Christ as the καινὴ κτίσις, then for Barth we must abolish Schleiermacher.

As we have just indicated, this act took place in the freedom of God and is not explained in terms of an evolutionary world process, e.g., as in the completion of human nature in the theology of Friedrich Schleiermacher to which we have just alluded. In addition, it has been suggested that it is not a necessity in the divine nature that God becomes man. That is:

> We can certainly say that we see the love of God to man originally grounded upon the eternal relation of God, Father and Son. But as this love is already free and unconstrained in God Himself, so, too, and only then rightly is it free in its realization towards man. That is, in His Word becoming flesh, God acts with inward freedom and not in fulfillment of a law to which he is supposedly subject.[21]

To put it another way, God is not duty-bound to His creation in any sense. That is: He is not bound because He is the Creator, nor is He duty-bound to call a halt to man's and the world's own self-destruction through sin by a new and fresh creation. In that we recognize that He has acted for us, we must also recognize His free good will in doing so and nothing else.

Further, when it is said that the Word became flesh, even in this state of becoming or having become, the Word is still free; the Word is still the sovereign Word of God. The fact that this event has occurred in no way restricts or contains the divine freedom. Indeed, strictly speaking, the Logos can never become the predicate or object in a sentence the subject of which is different from God. Thus while the statement "very God and very man"

-122-

signified an equation, it is not a reversible equation. If we do attempt this reversal, we will have to add that it is so because it has pleased very God to be very man, which, in effect, nullifies the reversal. In taking this position Karl Barth is again evidencing his indebtedness to the early Church, for not only does he call upon St. Anselm of Canterbury (whose limitations he acknowledges) and his celebrated Cur Deus Homo? which Barth sees as binding the incarnation to God's glory and man's impotence but also to St. Athanasius and Epiphanius. This concept of irreversibility is most succinctly put forth by the latter, according to Barth, when he remarked that "there is a primacy to the Logos from heaven who gave reality to the flesh in Him, the Logos Himself, and so bound the whole incarnation to Himself (εἰς ἑαυτόν , Adv. Haer. pan. 77, 29).[22]

The Word is the incarnate Word, i.e., the Word in the flesh and through the flesh, but nevertheless the Word and not the flesh. Barth states: "The Word is what He is even before and apart from His being flesh. Even as incarnate He derives His being to all eternity from the Father and from Himself, and not from the flesh."[23]

Donald M. Baillie, the late Scottish scholar of a few decades ago, in his classic essay on the doctrines of the incarnation and the atonement, made several criticisms of the position presented by Karl Barth. These statements or criticisms are in his consideration of the historical life of the incarnate Lord. Baillie suggests that Barth's theology has no real attachment to the Jesus of history; he writes:

> ...Barth tells us that the central text of the New Testament is John 1:14, 'The Word became flesh and dwelt among us;' but confesses also that in his early commentary on Romans,....he had failed to do justice to this central truth. One cannot help asking whether his theology has yet done justice to it.[24]

Baillie, as well as others, e.g., Otto piper and Martin Dibelius, continues by stating that Barth has reacted so violently against the "Jesus of history" movement that he does not seem interested in the historical Jesus at all. The point is made, rather, that "his theology has become so austerely a theology of the Word that...it is hardly a theology of the Word-made flesh."[25] In any case, on this account, Baillie's position is that Barth does not take the <u>incarnation</u> seriously.[26] He notes that Barth has no sympathy with the notion that the nature and character and purpose of God were reflected in, and thus revealed in, the human life and passion of Jesus Christ. Baillie even goes so far as to suggest that the emphasis in Christianity upon the teachings of Jesus Christ, especially about forgiveness and human sin, in view of the great emphasis in theological reflection upon Christology, do not usually intend to reduce His role to a teacher alone.[27]

In consideration of this criticism two comments would seem to be in order: first: it is quite true that Karl Barth does not seem to be enamoured by the Jesus of history; on this point we would have to agree with Donald Baillie (but we must also keep in mind the historical events that helped to shape the thought of Barth, namely, the failure, as he perceived it, of liberal Protestant theology to deal with the limitations of man and the greatness of God. See our chapter I). He does not proceed via a Jesus of history but proceeds from the presupposition of the Christological dogma, i.e., from the <u>revelation</u> of God in Jesus Christ. Second: it is argued that because Barth takes this approach and avoids or circumvents the historical Jesus, he does not truly have an incarnational theology. His Christology is viewed rather as a possible new monophysitism or as Baillie puts it, "a logotheism," because it is strictly the Word rather than the incarnation of the Son.

I think, however, that with respect to this latter point, we may legitimately raise the question: is the sole criterion for discussing the incarnation <u>absolutely</u> equated with the study of the resultant life as an historical phenomenon? Does the incarnation depend upon this? Barth does not seem to think so. The position he takes, however, is not necessarily one that abandons the gospel records.

On the contrary, recall that while Barth emphasizes the Easter message and the Easter faith, he also holds to the position that the Easter message and the Passion of our Lord, i.e., the entire life of Jesus, is the concrete content of the revelation which takes place at Easter (Cf. above, p. 114).

It is true that Barth places his emphasis upon the event of Jesus Christ as revealed in the resurrection and proceeds to work backward, but how can we, from the vantage point which we now occupy, i.e., from a post-resurrection position, really take a different course? Is it possible to exclude the phenomenon of the resurrection from our minds and from our experience and say that the nature, purpose and character of God is, without the total Biblical witness, revealed in the teaching of Jesus Christ? or, do we make these assertions because of the Easter story and the Easter faith? This does not mean to say, nor do I think that Barth means to say, there is no revelation in the life and teachings of Jesus. This would be clearly a misunderstanding and misrepresentation. Rather, what Barth says is that Jesus Christ, the Word made flesh is primary and all else, including the gospel accounts of His life and teachings are secondary in relation to Him. Nevertheless, Barth does not construct an abstract doctrine of Christ as one might suspect, but in a novel and interesting way he seeks to combine the Classical doctrine of the two natures and the Reformation doctrine of the two states. It is precisely in this way that the divinity of Christ is defined, so that it is not an abstract and a priori conception of the divine nature, but, in terms of the dynamic concept of humiliation and His humanity likewise in terms of exaltation. We shall speak of this more fully in the succeeding chapter.

2. The Word made flesh.

The second aspect ot the statement that the Word was made flesh means first and most generally that He became man, true and real man, participating in the same human nature and form and thus the same

-125-

historicity that we have. Herein lies the signifi-
cance of the second half of the answer to the
Christological question, i.e., _vere_ _Deus_ _vere_ _homo_.
Barth puts it in this way:

> God's revelation to us takes place in such
> a way that everything ascribable to man, his
> creaturely existence as an individually
> unique unity of body and soul in the time
> between birth and death, can now be predicated
> of God's eternal Son as well...everything
> miraculous about His being as a man derives
> its meaning and force from the fact that it
> concerns the true man Jesus Christ as a man
> like ourselves. This is especially true of
> the sign of His birth at the beginning, and
> the sign of the empty tomb at the end of
> His historical existence. It is true of
> the signs and wonders already manifested
> between this beginning and end, which pro-
> claim the Kingdom of God in its relation
> to the event of Easter. What in fact makes
> revelation revelation and miracle miracle
> is that the Word of God did actually become a
> real man and that therefore the life of this
> real man was the object and theatre of the
> acts of God, the light of revelation
> entering the world.[29]

Thus that the Word became _flesh_ indeed means that
He became a man. But Barth admonishes us to exercise care when we speak of this. For if we allow
that the Word became flesh, we must note that primarily this means not that He became a man but that
flesh implies human essence and existence, human
nature, _humanitas_, i.e., that which makes man man
as opposed to God, angel or animal. Thus Barth
states: "The Word became flesh means primarily and
of itself then that the Word became a participant
in human nature and existence. Human essence and
existence became His."[30]

One may receive the impression here that Jesus
was not at all a man but is really being conceived
of solely in generic terms. But Barth maintains that
this is not so for this participation in the human

-126-

essence and existence cannot be real except in the
concrete reality of one man, i.e., Jesus Christ.
Furthermore, he does not mean to state that Jesus
Christ "very God and very man" is tantamount to
Jesus Christ God and a man side by side, but that
the Son of God and therefore true God Himself is
also true man. Taking exception with some of the
Early Church Fathers, e.g., Gregory of Nyssa (Cat.
Or. 15f.), and following the line of thought expressed by John Calvin in his commentary on John 1:14,
and most especially in following the New Testament
itself, Barth argues that we stoop to level of
"religious" if we do not boldly assert Christ's
solodarity with us. Many religions, e.g., Buddhism,
Zoroastrianism, etc. have incarnations, but only
the New Testament declares that "He made Him to be
sin" (II Corinthians 5:21) and "He became a curse
for us." (Galatians 3:13)   Only in this understanding of incarnation do we have a strict concept of
Emmanuel -- God with us -- only here do we have a
real concept of revelation and reconciliation.
However, this man exists inasmuch as the Son of God
IS this man. The appropriation by the Word, not in
an Adoptionist sense, as if there had been a man
there and the Word became that man, of human essence
and existence, is the creation and preservation of
this man and therefore Christ's flesh. What is
added to the Word in the incarnation is not a secondary reality but His own work upon Himself,
which consists in the fact that He assumed human
nature.[31]

   This leads us to a conclusion similar to the
one reached about the divinity of Christ. We
noted under that heading that God is always subject
of the sentence, "The Word became flesh." We
must now note the same thing from the point of view
of His humanity. For we have just seen about that
the reality of Jesus Christ is that God Himself is
actively present in the flesh. If we read carefully
we may see a clear indication of the dynamic manner
in which Barth views the doctrine of the "two
natures" and the doctrine of the "two states." Barth
writes, in speaking of the Subject of the Word made
flesh, that:

...just because God is the Subject of it,
this being and acting are real. They are a
genuinely and truly human being and
acting. Jesus Christ is not a demi-god.
He is not an angel. Nor is He an ideal man.
He is man as we are, equal to us as creatures,
as a human individual, but also equal to us in
the state and condition into which our disobedience has brought us. And in being what
we are He is God's Word. Thus as one of us,
yet one of us Who is God's Word in person,
He represents God to us and He represents us
to God. In this way He is God's revelation
to us and our reconciliation with God.[32]

Thus we see that the Word is not only or not merely
the eternal Word but "flesh" as well, i.e., all that
we are and exactly like us even in our opposition to
Him. It is because of this that He makes contact
with us and is accessible for us. In this contact,
in this revelation, we meet the mystery of revelation,
i.e., the consummation of God's condescension,
and inconceivability, which is even greater than the
inconceivability of the combination of divine majesty
and human need.[33]

   While the Son of God is exactly as we are, yet
He is exactly as we are in quite a different way.
For what we do as sinful creatures He omits and
what we as sinful creatures omit He does. Barth insists that the Word assumes our human existence,
i.e., flesh; that He exists in the state and position,
under the curse and punishment of sinful man. That
is: He exists not only as a creature but as a sinful
creature in all remoteness from the Holy Creator.
This is what is meant by truly assuming our human
essence and existence and if He did not He would not
reach us or touch us and there would be no revelation, no reconciliation. We would still be in
our state and condition of remoteness. Our unholy
human existence is therefore hallowed since this
humanity has been adopted and assumed by the Word
of God Himself. We may ask, moreover, where and
how the sinlessness, the true humanity (for according
to Barth sin is not an attribute of true human exis-

tence as such), is made manifest. He does not
desire to present this in terms of his excellence
of character or virtue or good works, i.e., Christ
is not to be seen as the moral ideal, which we may
then emulate. Barth sees His sinlessness and His
obedience consisting in the one fact that He was
and willed to be God in the flesh, the divine
bearer of the burden which man as a sinner must
carry. In this connection he calls upon such
scriptural foundations as Philippians 2:8, "He
humbled Himself, by becoming obedient unto death,
even death on the cross." And also Mark 10:45,
"The Son of man came not to be ministered unto, but
to minister, and to give His life a ransom for
many." Thus we may see that Jesus' sinlessness
consists in His direct admission of the meaning of
the incarnation. That is: unlike Adam He does
not wish to be God, but rather in obedience before
God He acknowledges the state and position of
fallen man and He bears the wrath of God which
must fall upon this man, not as a fate, but as a
righteous necessary wrath. Put another way, He
takes the conditions, burdens and consequences of
alien humanity upon Himself. —

3. The Word became flesh.

This brings us to the final consideration of
this discussion, namely, that the "Word became
flesh." This points to the center of the mystery
which we have been describing and, therefore, may
very well be considered the decisive factor in
the Christological question. But problems are
obvious: how can the Word of God become without
surrendering His divinity? And, if He does not
surrender it, then what does becoming mean?
Barth maintains that there is a real becoming expressed "without the slightest surrender of the
divinity of the Word" and its "truth is that of a
miraculous act, an act of mercy on the part of
God."35 He supports this position by looking at
the results of an exegetical study of the context
of John 1:14. That is to say: since, "becoming"
is ascribed to His creatures as distinct from Him
the Creator, there is nothing we expect to hear

-129-

less than He, too, is Himself the subject of an
$\overset{?}{\epsilon}\gamma\overset{\prime}{\epsilon}\nu\epsilon\tau o$ and that He too can exist in the same way
as the things created by Him. Furthermore, we
must recall what we have already said: (1) that his
becoming is an act of the Word Who is Lord and (2)
that humanity, from its own side, has no capacity,
nor worthiness or power by which it may become the
humanity of the Word.[36]

Barth suggests that our difficulty may be
arrested, or at least clarified, if we paraphrase
the statement "the Word became flesh" to read "the
Word assumed flesh." In this way Barth sees a
protection against the notion that in the incarnation
the Word ceases to be entirely Himself equal to
Himself. This is, indeed, an impossibility for
God cannot cease to be God. This is, the astonishing
factor, the inconceivable factor, that in taking
over human nature, in assuming human nature, God
brought humanity into unity with Himself, i.e., as
His own predicate along with His original predicate
of divinity.

Sometimes a misunderstanding occurs with respect
to Jesus As Mediator, i.e., whether He is really
a third nature and neither God nor man at all. Here
again Barth points out that the paraphrase, "the
Word assumed flesh," acts as a safeguard. Barth
states:

> It is not the divine nature that acts where
> God acts. It is the Triune God in His divine
> nature, one in three modes of existence of
> Father, Son and Holy Spirit. So, too, in this
> assumption of human being by the eternal Word....
> The unity into which the human nature is assumed
> is thus unity with the Word...the union of the
> human with the divine nature. But the eternal
> Word is with the Father and Holy Spirit the
> unchangeable God Himself and so incapable of
> any change or admixture. Unity with Him, the
> "becoming" of the Word, cannot therefore mean
> the origination of a third between Word and
> Flesh, but only the assumption of the flesh
> by the Word.[37]

Thus the unity of God and man in Christ is, then, the act of the Word in becoming or the act of the Word in assuming human being. What is proclaimed in this unity is this: this man Jesus Christ is identical with God because the Word became flesh, and as we have already seen He lost nothing but was yet the eternal Word. However, because He became flesh, Barth indicates that He then not only lives through God and with God, but He Himself is God. Nor is He autonomous and self-existent. His reality, existence and being is wholly and absolutely that of God Himself, the God Who acts in His Word. His manhood is only the predicate of His Godhead, or better put, it is only the predicate of His Godhead, or better put, it is only the predicate assumed in inconceivable condescension of the Word acting upon us, the Word Who is Lord.

At this point, let us make two comments. These are in reference to Barth's treatment of this subject, i.e., the Word made flesh. First: as we consider his conception of the humanity of the Word made flesh, we are left with the impression that the human situation, the human condition, is so completely expurgated by the flesh-assumption of the Word that the subjective is swallowed up in this event, in the Word's taking human nature upon Himself, that is, in the objective. In this event there is a removal of sin to be sure, but in its removal all else seems to be discarded as well. There is no longer a need for forgiveness, for guilt has been removed. Indeed we may even go so far as to suggest that man himself has been removed.

Second: even though Barth attempts to give full consideration to the humanity of Christ, even though he does for a fact lay great emphasis upon this aspect of the nature of Christ, even though he contends that the incarnation is not a kenosis of divinity but rather the authentication of the Godhead, an act of obedience to the essential nature of God, yet even here, despite all the effort and intention to the contrary, the humanity

-131-

seems to be purely instrumental. It was only from
the perspective of His divinity that His human
passion derived its uniqueness. God is the Subject,
as we have seen, of the flesh and because He is the
Subject of a real human being, this being is
real.[38] But if it is only the divine Who is able
to detach us from our sin and nothingness, is there
any real necessity for Him to become man and endure
humiliation and subject Himself to juridicial pain
and procedure?[39] We shall return to these criticisms in our critique of Barth's conception of
reconciliation later. At the present time we conclude our analysis and brief commentary on Barth's
understanding of the Classical Christology here and
proceed to analyze the unique and interesting manner
in which he combines it with the Reformation doctrine
of the "two states" in Volume IV of the Church Dogmatics where he presents his doctrine of Reconciliation.

CHAPTER 6 NOTES

1. Karl Barth, Church Dogmatics, Volume I/2, "The Doctrine of the Word of God," translated by G.T. Thomson and Harold Knight (Edinburgh: T. & T. Clark, 1956), p. 122.

2. Ibid., p. 123.

3. Ibid., pp. 123-124.

4. Ibid., pp. 122, 124.

5. Ludwig Feuerbach in his Essence of Christianity (1841) explained God, psychologically, as a projection of man's desires and needs, thus anticipating and influencing later critiques of religion by Karl Marx and Sigmund Freud. In Feuerbach's view, all theology was anthropology.

6. Barth, op. cit., p. 125.

7. Ibid.

8. Ibid., p. 131.

9. Ibid.

10. Ibid., p. 132.

11. Ibid. One, of course, could argue this point. Why is this Christological formula central? Why not one of the earlier synoptic or Pauline formulae? if, indeed, they are formulae at all?

12. Ibid., pp. 13-14.

13. Ibid., p. 15.

14. We should note the affinity between the doctrine by calling attention to the fact that the basic doctrine of the Trinity is formulated by reflection and analysis of the basic statement "God reveals Himself." Likewise the Christological confession is an analysis, giving answer to the basic question of who Jesus Christ is. Cf. Church Dogmatics,

Volume I/2, pp. 1-25. Also cf. George S. Hendry, The Gospel of the Incarnation (Philadelphia: The Westminster Press, 1958), p. 99.

15. Barth, Church Dogmatics, Volume I/2, p. 15.

16. Ibid., pp. 23-24.

17. Karl Barth, Church Dogmatics, Volume II/1, "The Doctrine of God" (Edinburgh: T & T Clark, 1957), p. 25.

18. Barth, Church Dogmatics, Volume I/2, p. 132.

19. Ibid., p. 134.

20. Ibid., p. 134.

21. Ibid., p. 135.

22. Ibid., p. 136.

23. Ibid.

24. Donald M. Baillie, God was in Christ (New York: Charles Scribners Sons, 1948), pp. 53, 61.

25. Ibid.

26. As noted by George S. Hendry in The Gospel of the Incarnation, p. 34.

27. Baillie, op. cit., p. 37.

28. Ibid., p. 53. Cf. Hendry, op. cit., pp. 34-35.

29. Barth, Church Dogmatics, Volume I/2, p. 147.

30. Ibid., p. 149.

31. Ibid., pp. 147-150.

32. Ibid., p. 151. There are echoes here of that famous phrase used by both Athanasius and Irenaeus, "He became what we are in order that we might become what He is."

33. We noted earlier that Barth had more sympathy with the Classical Christological formulations than with modern concepts. Here we may see an attempt on his part to improve upon the Patristic conception of the humanity of Christ in ontological terms. The earlier position, against which objections have been frequently raised, conceived of Christ's humanity not merely as individual, but as generic or universal; its assumption was meant not that He became a man like other men, but that He entered into an ontological relation with mankind as a whole, a position which enabled the Fathers to maintain that the work of Christ was done for man in man prior to its appropriation by man and thus to establish an objective ground for the work of Christ in its vicarious character. Barth similarly states that Christ took human nature upon Himself, but unlike the Fathers states that He became exactly as we are, and indeed, herein lies, however inconceivable, the revelation of God. In both cases, however, there is a difficulty in the relationship of the objective reality and the subjective appropriation of the event.

34. Barth, Church Dogmatics, Volume I/2, pp. 155ff.

35. Ibid., p. 159.

36. Traditionally, this latter point was the error of the Adoptionists and the Arians.

37. Barth, Church Dogmatics, Volume I/2, p. 161.

38. Ibid., p. 151.

39. Although Barth does not approach the problem of Christology by way of the Jesus of history, he does wrestle quite substantially with the incarnation and in so doing has brought new illumination to this ancient problem, even if he at the same time has not alleviated all of our problems and difficulties, and, perhaps, has even created some new ones of his own.

CHAPTER VII

AN ANALYSIS OF KARL BARTH'S CHRISTOLOGY

IN VOLUME IV

SEEN IN THE LIGHT OF

THE DOCTRINE OF RECONCILIATION

A. RECASTING THE CHRISTOLOGICAL NATURES IN THE
   CHRISTOLOGICAL STATES

It is of importance to restate/summarize the
manner in which Karl Barth formulates his Christology. The person and the work of Christ are seen
as a unity which cannot be divided. The being of
Jesus Christ is the history of the unity of the
living God and the living man, the content of
which history is reconciliation. Thus Barth
writes what is a real recapitulation of his position:

> And what takes place in this history (unity
> of God and man), and therefore in the being
> of Christ as such, is atonement. Jesus Christ
> is not what He is--very God, very man, very
> God-man--in order as such to mean and do and
> accomplish something else which is atonement.
> But His being as God and man and God-man con-
> sists in the completed act of reconciliation
> of man with God.[1]

That which takes place in this history is the
humbling of the deity in that He becomes man, the
condescension of the Eternal Son of the Eternal
Father; and the exaltation of man to the side of
God, for in that God became like man, so man became
like God, i.e., he is exalted by the humiliation
of God.

In Barth, then, the classical doctrine of the
two natures and the Reformation concept of the
states of humiliation and exaltation have been
brought together in a way that marks innovation,
for instead of seeing humiliation and exaltation
as two successive states, i.e., His state of
humiliation followed by His state of exaltation;
he sees them as two sides or directions of what
took place in Jesus Christ for the reconciliation
of man with God. This is His being--humiliation
and exaltation---the actuality of Jesus Christ as
the very God Who humbles Himself and the man who
is exalted.[2]

The fact that Jesus Christ is the active subject in this history, that in Him the humiliated God and the exalated man are one, that He is the God-man, means that He Himself attests to the reconciliation that takes place in this event of humiliation; He is the pledge of it in His existence, its actuality, the truth of it that speaks out, and in this consists His prophetic office and its implications for the anthropological sphere in terms of man's calling, the sending of the community and the hope of the Christian man. It is in Jesus Christ Himself that man's justification, sanctification, and calling is true and actual, and therefore applicable to all men. "In the Christian there is an appropriation of the grace of God ascribed to all men in Jesus Christ, a subjective apprehension of what has been done for the whole world in the happening of the atonement."3

The unity of Christology and reconciliation here means that in Jesus Christ we encounter the reconciling God and reconciled man and with both in their unity. "As this One He is the subject of the act of reconciliation between God and all men."4 The event of the cross is then the fulfilled reconciliation accomplished by the humiliation or condescension of the Son and revealed in the resurrection. In viewing Christology and reconciliation in this way, i.e., by bracketing the person and the work and by interpreting the person by the work and vice versa, Barth reaches back behind orthodoxy to the Reformation and behind the Christology of the Early Church to the New Testament. Further, this interpretation avoids the subordinating of the person to the work and having a purely functional Christology on the one hand, and avoids isolating the person from the work in favor of an ontology of Christ's being, on the other. The former is a polemic primarily against Rudolf Bultmann and the latter against the form of traditional Christology.

B. THE HUMILIATION OF GOD IN HIS BECOMING MAN

The first aspect of reconciliation, which we will consider, concerns the humiliation of the vere

-140-

Deus in His becoming man, the movement which Barth
describes under the heading "Jesus Christ, The Lord
as Servant," and more precisely under the section:
"The Obedience of the Son of God." This latter
section (59) is in turn subdivided into three sub-
sections: "The way of the Son of God in a far
country," or the doctrine of the deity of Christ;
"The Judge judged in our place," or the doctrine
of that which God does in becoming flesh; and
"The Verdict of the Father," which serves as a
transitional section in that it establishes a
positive relation between the Christological and
anthropological spheres through a consideration
of the resurrection.

The substance of Barth's thought on the deity
of Jesus Christ is found in the assertion, namely,
that the deity of Jesus Christ is to be found
exactly in His act of obedience to the Father,
in the humbling of Himself and becoming man. Contrary to traditional dogmatics which views the
incarnation of the Son as a temporary parenthesis
in His exalted and majestic and transcendent
being as God, Barth would have us see His deity
in no other place than in His becoming man, in His
journey into the far country.[5] Thus it is necessary
to confess and to affirm not only the deity of
Christ but the very extraordinary way in which it
is known. The mystery of Christ's existence consists in the identity of the majesty of God ---
not in obvious splendor, but rather in the opposite.
In this sense when the New Testament speaks of
Lordship, it speaks also of obedience which is
manifest in humiliation, suffering and lowliness
of this Jesus --- identified with sinners, crucified
and buried.

At this point Barth is rigorously applying a
fundamental assertion he has made throughout his
dogmatics on the nature of revelation, i.e., that
God is in His revelation none other than He is in
Himself, that in His opus ad extra He is none other
than He is in the event of His inner being.[6] With
this presupposition, the bold description of the
deity of Christ is made necessary, for that which

-141-

characterizes the life of Jesus Christ is "the fact
that in relation to God and therefore to the world
as well, this man wills only to be obedient--
obedient to the will of the Father, which is done
on earth for the redemption of man as it is done in
heaven."[7] This apparent contradiction to the being
of God is that which precisely distinguishes the
man Jesus as the Son of God.

This obedience of Jesus Christ is not simply
seen in His becoming man, but His becoming flesh,
His identifying Himself with sinful humanity, and
existing under the wrath and judgment of the elect-
ing and loving God, affirming the divine sentence
on man and allowing it to be fulfilled on Him. It
is the giving of this condescending, this humbling
in this way, that is the mystery of the deity of
Jesus Christ. Barth states: "(1) the obedience
of the Son to the Father, shown (2) in His self-
humiliation, His way into the far country, fulfilled
in His death on the cross. It is in these two
moments and their combination, that there is en-
closed the mystery that He is very God and of the
divine nature. It is a mystery because true being
as God and in the divine nature is His alone of
all men and all creatures."[8]

There is no other alternative for Barth than
to see the deity of Christ in His obedience, for
to do otherwise would be to speak of His act of
humiliation as something outside of His being;
it would mean that in the incarnation there was a
de-divinization of God. This would simply rob
the statement "God was in Christ" of any positive
meaning whatsoever. To say that God is truly and
altogether in Christ "tells us that God for His
part is God in His unity with this creature, this
man, in His human and creaturely nature without
ceasing to be God, without any alteration or
diminution of His Divine nature."[9]

When one accepts this alternative, he is left
with two possibilities of viewing the incarnation:
(1) either as an absolute paradox noetically and
ontically, i.e., as a new mystery or (2) of seeing
that God is true to Himself in this condescension.

For Barth this latter alternative is the only real choice open for:

> we begin with the insight that God is "not a God of confusion, but of Peace" (I Corinthians 14:33). In Him there is no paradox, no antinomy, no division, no inconsistency, not even the possibility of it....What He is and does He is and does in full unity with Himself that He is also - and especially above all - in Christ, that He becomes a creature, man, flesh, that He enters into our being in contradiction, that He takes up Himself its consequences.[10]

He is the Father of lights with Whom there is no variableness nor interplay of light and darkness (James 1:17).

The traditional views of God's immutability must be slashed open in order to include this possibility in His unalterable being. He states: "we may believe that God can and must only be absolute in contrast to all that is relative, exalted in contrast to all that is lowly, etc., in short that He can and must be only the 'Wholly Other.' But such beliefs are shown to be quite untenable, and corrupt and pagan, by the fact that God does in fact be and do this in Jesus Christ."[11] God is infinite, exalted, active, impassible, transcendent, but He is all this in such a way as Lord that He embraces the opposites of these concepts even while He is superior to them. Consequently, God can act towards the world "in an absolute way and also a relative way, in an infinite way and also a finite, in an exalted and also a lowly, in an active and also a passive, in a transcendent and also an immanent, and finally in a divine and also a human - indeed, in relation to which He Himself can become worldly, making His own both its form, the forma servi and also its cause, and all without giving up His own form, the forma Dei, and His own glory, but adopting the form and cause of man into the most perfect communion with His own, accepting solidarity with the world."[12] God can do this because He is all this as Lord.

-143-

But this fact, that God acts in this way ad
extra is, as we have stated before, grounded in the
fact that He is this in Himself, and so we go on
to say, "that for God it is just as natural to be
lowly as it is to be high, to be near as it is to
be far, to be little as it is to be great, to be
abroad as it is to be home."[13] The truth and
actuality of our atonement depends on the fact that
as God exists and speaks and acts in Jesus Christ,
He exists and speaks out as the One He was from
all eternity and will be to all eternity. From
the fact that the true God is the acting Subject,
which is necessitated by the fact that: "In matters
of atonement of the world with God the world itself
cannot act - for it is a world which is at enmity
with God, which stands in need of reconciliation
with Him. It cannot act even in the form of a
supreme and best being produced by it and belonging
to it. Anyone other or less than true God is not
a legitimate subject competent to act in this matter."[14]
The presence of, and action of, Jesus Christ is
the presence and action of God Himself and truly
Himself in His acting and intervening in the world,
i.e., "as the credo,...we have to follow the New
Testament in understanding the presence and action
of God in Jesus Christ as the most proper and direct
and immediate presence and action of the one true
God in the sphere of human and world history."[15]
From these considerations one must accept the
humiliation and lowliness and supremely the obedience
of Christ as the one dominating moment in our conception of God.[16] Obedience and suffering are
not an option, rather they are the one and only way
for the Son of God. "He is a suffering servant
who wills this profoundly unsatisfactory being, who
will anything other in the obedience in which He
shows Himself the Son of God."[17] On this point,
Berthold Klappert concludes that Barth's central
thesis is that "the character of the whole history
of Jesus Christ as the history of humiliation on the
cross is the center from which he interprets the
early Christian confession of the duty of Jesus."[18]
Here, furthermore, on the cross the Son of God
reveals Himself as the One He is. This suggests
that Barth understands the incarnation not in a

-144-

traditional manner at all, but rather from the Cross. This is, however, a misunderstanding of Barth, for he repeatedly speaks of the incarnation in the Church Dogmatics, IV/1,2 and as it relates to the atonement (cf. C.D. IV/2, pp. 36-116). It is never Barth's intention, in our judgment, to separate John 1:14 from II Corinthians 5:19, as Klappert would like to suggest. Incarnation, which means God's coming as man, and reconciliation, which deals with what happens when He comes, are two sides of the ONE action or movement of God in Jesus Christ.

In interpreting the New Testament in this manner and in keeping with his basically Chalcedonian Christology developed earlier in the Church Dogmatics, Barth reaffirms, asserts, insists even, that by becoming very man or true man, God did not cease to be God. While God did not need the otherness of the world, and therefore man, it is, nevertheless, precisely in this condescension that deity is revealed. Consequently, we are prohibited from speculating about the deity of God apart from this revelation in Jesus Christ. In the incarnation of the Son, we are confronted with the Lord Who became a servant. God shows His nature as the One Who loves in freedom in His condescension in His Son. God is able to do this and this He does. He becomes in other words Deus pro nobis - a partner with man, a brother of man, in order to save his wayward creature and covenant partner. Concerning this Barth states quite concretely:

> Deus pro nobis means simply that God has
> not abandoned the world and man in the
> unlimited need of his situation, but
> that He wills to hear this need as His
> own, that He took it upon Himself, and
> that He cries with man in this need.[19]

Therefore, in God Himself, there is an above and a below, a prius and a posterius, a superiority and a subordination. However, rather than this being a denial of His unity, His unity consists precisely in the fact that He is both the One Who is obeyed and another who obeys. God did not need the otherness

of the world and man, i.e., in order not to be alone
God did not need to posit any creature; He did not
need co-existence with the creature. He does not
out of necessity posit the creature, but rather,
in freedom as the basic act of His grace; His entire
relationship to that which is outside of Himself
rests upon this fact.[20]

G. C. Berkouwer raises several questions concerning this aspect of Barth's conception of the
doctrine of reconciliation. Suffice it for us just
to raise them at this point and discuss them more
fully in the succeeding chapter. In raising these
questions Berkouwer is quite explicit that Barth
himself is aware, also, that he raises profound
questions. Berkouwer states that the concept of
"obedience assumes an 'above and a 'below' and
seems, therefore, to endanger the unity of the
divine being."[21] We may then ask, "Can the one
God command and also be obedient? Can command
and obedience co-exist within the reality of the
one true God."[22]

The problem that is posed by this seeming contradiction in the being of God, i.e., this above and
below, this command and obedience, is solved by
Barth, by the fact that God is more than One Who
rules in majesty and obeys in humility, but that He
is also a Third, the One Who affirms the One and
equal God-head through and by and in the two modes
of being, i.e., the Holy Spirit makes possible and
maintains His fellowship with Himself as the One and
the Other. Thus God is One, Whose Godhead consists
in this history, Who is in these three modes of
being the One God, Eternal, the One Who loves in His
freedom and is free in His Love. As Barth states
it:

> The one God is both the One and the Other.
> And, we continue, He is the one and the other
> without any cleft or differentiation but in
> perfect unity and equality because in the
> same perfect unity and equality He is also a
> Third, the One who affirms the one and equal
> Godhead through and by the two modes of

being,....In virtue of this third mode of
being He is in the other two without distinction or contradiction, the Whole God
in each.[23]

It is significant to point out that Barth is not
describing any abstract concept of deity, Trinity
or incarnation, but rather concrete event/concrete
history. He charges any neutral Godhead as being
empty, an illusion by which men are fooled into
believing that they have reached the acme of
religion and philosophy. However, for Barth the
only place to find the deity is in history (i.e.,
his-story).

In the act of reconciliation, in this history,
God becomes what He has not previously been, taking
into unity with Himself a creaturely and sinful
being. But this act has its basis in His own inner
being, in His own life and it is done "as the
strangely logical final continuation of the history
in which He is God."[24] That is: He can enter in
Himself precisely because He is Himself the One Who
rules and commands in majesty, but also in His
divine person, the One Who is obedient and humble.
He is simply activating and revealing Himself ad
extra in the world. "He is in time what He is in
eternity (and what He can be also in time because
of His eternal being)....He is in our lowliness
what He is in His majesty and what He can be also
in our lowliness because His majesty is also lowliness."[25]

In seeing the relation of the Father and the
Son as that of majesty and humility, of an above
and a below, etc., Barth seems also to bring into
focus a point made earlier, i.e., that in God's
own being and life there is grace.[26] From this
perspective Barth sees the relation of the Father
and the Son reflected analogically in the relation
of the Creator and the creature and in the deity
and the humanity of Jesus Christ. This is clearly
brought out in the subsection on the resurrection
of Jesus Christ which is described as purely the
action of God the Father in which the Son is

wholly object:

> Certainly in the resurrection of Jesus Christ
> we have to do with a movement and action that
> took place not merely in human history but
> first and foremost in God Himself a movement
> and action in which Jesus Christ as the Son of
> God had no less part than in His humiliation
> to the death of the cross, yet only as a pure
> object and recipient of the grace of God.
> We must not be afraid of this apparently
> difficult thought that as in God Himself
> (as we have seen), in the relationship of the
> Son to the Father (the model of all that is
> demanded from man by God), there is a pure
> obedience, subordination and subjection, so
> too in the relationship of the Father to the
> Son (the model of all that is given to man
> by God), there is a free and pure grace which
> as such can only be received, and the histori-
> cal fulfillment of which is the resurrection
> of Jesus Christ.27

In discussing Barth's recasting of the two natures
in conjunction with the two states, we may raise
the question, in Anselmic terms, Cur Deus Homo?
It is correct to say this because God did this as
an outward activation and revelation of the inward
riches of His deity. God so acts "that the world
created by Him might have and see within it, in the
Son as the image of the Father, its own original,
that wills it and does it for the sake of His glory
in the world, to confirm and proclaim His will
not to be without the world, not to be God in isolation."28

     But the purpose of God in so humbling Himself
is for the sake of man --- propter nos homines et
propter nostram salutem. He acts in the midst of
a world that is on its way to the abyss. In His
Son God takes to Himself the radical neediness
of the world, doing for it what it cannot do for
itself, arresting and reversing its fatal course to
the abyss. This is an act of God's freedom; it must
be stressed that it is not a necessary act, nor
does God owe this to the world or Himself. Never-

theless, He is God pro nobis, i.e., He is God for us.

Let us proceed further, under this caption of
humiliation, to make some brief observations concerning this statement, e.g., how far He is for us,
how He has taken up our cause and how He has saved
man from sin.

(1) God accomplished this by taking upon Himself the place and status of man, his situation,
making it his own situation. This has several implications: Jesus Christ in taking upon Himself the
human situation, i.e., human creatureliness and
human nature, fully becomes a creature, He stands
with men in mortal need; He participates in the
being of the world; there is no reservation with
respect to His solidarity with us. "He did become---
and this is the presupposition of all that follows---
the brother of man, harrassed and assaulted with
him, with him in the stream which hurries downward
to the abyss, hastening with him to death, to the
cessation of being and nothingness."[29] Very simply
this means that God has not abandoned the world or
man in the moment of need.

(2) Since man is sinful man, man alienated from
God, God in taking the human situation means that
He stands in solidarity with sinful man, i.e., His
becoming subject to the temptation in which man
suffers and in which he becomes a sinner and the
enemy of God. He faced the "impossible possibility,"
that which God had not willed, and yet which assaults
man, and He knew its power and strength as no other
man. "He was not immune from sin. He did not commit
it, but He was not immune from it. In this respect,
too, He became the brother of man. He did not
float over the situation like a being of a completely
different kind. He entered into it as a man with
men."[30] What takes place is this: the being of the
Son takes the place of man and acts for man. That
is: man's situation of alienation from God is met
by removing the alien, and putting in his place,
i.e., in the situation of alienation, One Who is
actually one with God and Who now faces and acts for
those who are alienated.

-149-

(3) While God came into our human situation
as our brother identifying Himself with us in order
to change the status of man and the world, He also
came as "Judge of the World and every man." That
is: "He is the Saviour of the World insofar as
in a very definite (and most astonishing way) He is
also its Judge."[31] He comes to judge the world,
but "to show His grace in the execution of His
judgment, to pronounce us free in passing sentence,
to free us by imprisoning us, to ground our life
on our death, to redeem us and save us from our
destruction. This is how God has actually judged
us in Jesus Christ."[32]

This leads Barth to answer the question of how
this strange judgment, this saving work, took place.
"What took place is that the Son of God fulfilled
the righteous judgment on us men by Himself taking
our place as man and in our place undergirding the
judgment under which we passed...." In this way,
in the "for us" He was our Judge against us.
"Everything happens to us as it had to happen,
but because God willed to execute His Judgment upon
us in His Son it all happened in His person, as
His accusation and condemnation and destruction.
He judged and it was the Judge who was judged and
let Himself be judged."[33]

While His humanity let Him be judged like us,
His divinity gave Him the competence and power to
allow this to happen to Him and the authority to
pronounce us righteous on the ground of that which
happened to Him.

In His doing this for us, in His taking to
Himself, - to fulfill all righteousness -
our accusation and condemnation and
punishment, in His suffering in our place
and for us, there came to pass our reconciliation with God. Cur Deus homo? In
order that God as man might do and accomplish
and achieve and complete all this for us
wrong-doers, in order that in this way there
might be brought about by Him our reconciliation with Him and conversion to Him.[34]

This seems to be the very heart of Barth's
teaching on the work of Jesus Christ and we may see
why for him the reconciliation of the world cannot
be understood as a mere possibility calling for
actualization in the life of the believer.   In
Christ took place the strange judgment which means
the pardon and redemption of man: "it took place
in Him, in the one man, and therefore there and
then, _illic et tunc_, and in significance _hic et nunc_,
for us in our modern here and now."[35] It cannot
disappear or be dissolved in favor of its significance, it can and must be taken as that which is
significant in its significance and therefore in
and for itself as the history of Jesus Christ as
it took place there and then, and as it can be
recounted: that is, how it happened for us.[36]

        In that Barth sees that the deity of Christ
is precisely in the event of humiliation, as the
Son of God in the far country, as the Judge judged
in our place, he is understanding the classical
Christological formulation in a slightly different
manner, i.e., as we have already indicated, his
concern is not to view the _vere Deus_ abstractly.
For we cannot first know his deity, i.e., His
omnipotence and majesty, and then later come to an
understanding of His humiliation. On the contrary,
it is exactly here, as we have attempted to describe, in His humiliation, that the essence of
his deity appears: _vere Deus_. "Here we have a
powerful concern...to see together what traditional
dogmatics had always separated, the God-man and the
humanity of God."[37] This modification replaces the
idea of succession in the humiliation -- exaltation
relationship by the idea of contemporaneity.   In
this intertwining of the doctrine of the two
natures and the doctrine of the two states, a
synthetic relationship between the humiliation of
God and the exaltation of man is established. It
is in this event that reconciliation takes place:
"in and for itself, in and through the existence
of One Who acts and suffers in it and therefore objectively for us, this Gospel story is the story
of redemption."[38]

All considerations, which make it compatible with
God's honor and with His being to speak of God's
self-humiliation, self-surrender, suffering,
humility and obedience, arise, according to Barth,
from an a priori God-concept which is set as our norm
for reflection about God. In this manner, we do not
take a radically Christocentric position, i.e., we
do not then take our point of departure from the
reality of the revelation in Jesus Christ Who is
not only truly man, but also the One Who is truly
God. In a natural theology God-concept, it is not
possible to make such predications about God, the
esse absolutum cannot suffer and be obedient, but
this has nothing to do with Christian theology.
We come to a wholly different view, in the opinion
of Karl Barth, when we think of God in terms of
Christ. God reveals Himself as He is in Himself
in Jesus Christ. The confession of Christ's true
deity, then, silences the objections of reason which
would determine what is or what is not possible
for God. When these objections are silenced, we
no longer see God as a high and unemotional being,
in abstracto, but we see the humble self-surrender-
ing God. He is the true God in the suffering and
obedience of Christ. He is God in humiliation,
true God in humiliation.

C. THE EXALTATION OF THE SON OF MAN

In the second part of this fourth volume Karl
Barth turns to a more specific study of the man
reconciled to God in the event of reconciliation.
We have seen, in the preceding analysis, that the
first part of this volume was to clarify the dynamic
concept of humiliation, the mighty condescension of
God, the obedience of the Son. Now Barth seeks to
develop the objective basis for man's participation
in this event of reconciliation, for this is as
much a part of the event as the divine condescension that calls it forth. Barth's thought on this
problem, may perhaps, best be seen in a quotation
from the opening pages of this volume:

Now what was done for man, and the meaning

for him of the divine atonement and therefore of the grace of God, is that, as God
condescends and humbles Himself to man, and
becomes man, man himself if exalted, not as
God or like God, but to God, being placed
at His side, not in identity, but in true
fellowship with Him, and becoming a new man
in this exaltation and fellowship. It is true
enough that the atonement is wholly and
utterly a movement from above to below, of
God to man. But it is also true that this
truth encloses the further truth that the
atonement is wholly and utterly a movement
from below to above, the movement of reconciled man to God.[39]

Thus in the structure of Karl Barth's doctrine of
reconciliation, in and with and at the same time
as there takes place the humiliation of God,
there takes place the exaltation, the raising up
of the Son of Man. Or, put another way, in Jesus
Christ the covenant has been fulfilled from both
sides. In Him, the covenant-making God and the
covenant-keeping man are one. He is the man exalted
by the grace of God. This issue of great importance
here is the extreme objectivity with which Barth
develops the thought. Even as in the humiliation
of the Son of God Who was judged in our place, our
sinful being was removed from us in actuality apart
from any human response so in the exaltation of
the Son of Man, there also takes place our exaltation to fellowship with God as an actuality apart
from our response to it.

In speaking of the vere homo of Jesus Christ,
Barth does not mean to refer to Him as one who
partakes of human nature known by us, but that He
Himself defines human nature, that a genuine
knowledge of man can only be based on a particular
knowledge of Him. As the true man He differs
from us, in that His existence is also that of the
Son of God, there also took place in His history
an exaltation of the humanity which is common to
Him and to all men.[40] "In His person, as the
humanitas of this man, humanitas itself is set in

-153-

motion - from here to there, from the far country
to which the Subject who acts here as man, the Son
of God, gave Himself, back again to the home which
is shown to be the home of man by the fact that the
One who came from it willed to become and be
the Son of Man, and to which every man may really
return, and has already done so, in the person of
this One."[41] He completely contradicts the course
of man's life, affirming the grace of God, being
the man well-pleasing to God and thus exalting
the essence of man into a completely different
sphere. The following seems to point up Barth's
true meaning. Since Jesus of Nazareth is an
empirical human being, a human figure, He is not
at all inacessible, yet Barth adds:

> It is one thing to know, another to recog-
> nize. To recognize is to know Him as the
> One He -- and He alone is, as the One in
> Whom,...there takes place and is that which
> is new and unique in the series of all other
> elements and figures in cosmic being and
> history -- the fact that without ceasing to
> be the Creator, the Creator Himself also
> becomes a creature, and therefore without
> ceasing to be God, God also becomes man. To
> know Him as this -- just this, no more no
> less -- is to recognize Him. But as this
> He obviously does not belong to the sphere
> of what we can see and interpret...As a man,
> He is certainly an element or figure of cosmic
> being and its history with a cosmic nature.
> But beyond this He is also -- He alone --
> the Creator, God Himself Who has His ground
> of being in the fact that this new and
> absolutely unique thing takes'place in Him....
> Recognition of this man can obviously only
> take place as a new act of cognition, i.e.,
> one which shares in the newness of His being.[42]

Barth, in discussing the exaltation of the
Son of Man, does so in the theological contexts of
election, incarnation, resurrection and ascension.
However, for our purposes, we shall confine our
remarks to those relating to the incarnation.

In reference to the incarnation itself, Barth's
emphasis, as we have noted, is on the sovereignty,
initiative and freedom of God in this event. In
that it is the nature of the true God to be humble,
in His mode as the Son, He wills and becomes the
human partner of the covenant as well as its Lord;
He keeps it from man's side as well as from God's
side. In this act in which God takes the humanity
into union with Himself Barth employs the traditional
concepts of an-hypostasia and en-hypostasia, i.e.,
there is no actuality in union with the Son of God --
as being unavoidable if one is to describe the
mystery correctly. Moreover, that which the Son
assumed into unity with Himself was not merely "a
man,"

> ...but the humanum, the being and essence,
> the nature and kind which is that of all
> men and which characterizes them all as
> men, and distinguishes them from other
> creatures. It is not the idea of humanum,
> in which per definitionem, this could exist
> in real men and either never and nowhere or
> only always and everywhere. It is the con-
> crete possibility of the existence of the
> one man in a specific form - a man elected
> and prepared for this purpose, not by him-
> self, but by God....But in this form it is
> that which is human in all men. [43]

Thus His existence has a relevance for all men,
for it is not merely one man, but the humanum of all
men which is posited and exalted as such to unity
with God. [44]

This unity between the Son of God and the Son
of Man is stressed by Barth in very emphatic terms.
The existence of the Son of God became and is the
existence of a man; He became the Thou of the One
Eternal God. There are not two existing side by
side or even within one another. There is but one
God the Son and nothing, therefore, either alongside or within Him. But this One exists, not only
in His divine nature but also in human being and
essence, in our nature and kind. [45] God Himself

speaks, acts, and suffers when this man speaks, and
acts, and suffers. This is why His history has the
great significance that it does for us, for God
Himself is the acting Subject here. It is the deity
of Jesus Christ that gives Him His significance, that
allows Him to do His saving work and do it completely
and perfectly.

> The human speaking and acting and suffering
> and triumphing of this one man concerns us
> all, and His history is our history of salva-
> tion which changes the human situation, just
> because God Himself is its human Subject in
> His Son, just because God Himself came into
> this world in His Son, and as one of us "a
> guest this world of ours He trod."[46]

The Son of God really participates in human essence,
He unites His person, that which by definition cannot be united, and in this union neither is destroyed. Both the humiliation of the divine and the
exaltation of the human retain their designation
as divine and human in this union, not changing
one into another.

With this Barth moves to his central concern,
namely, that in this union the Son of God exalted
human essence into Himself and as very God became
very man.[47] In Jesus Christ our human essence
conjoined with the divine essence. But Barth is
quick to point out that this does not mean that
the two elements are in simple correspondence. That
is to say, His humiliation as the Son of God is
that He becomes man, but His exaltation as the Son
of Man is not that He has become God. Barth puts
it in these terms:

> The human essence of the Son of God will
> always be human essence, although united
> with His divine essence, and therefore
> exalted in and by Him, set at the side of
> the Father, brought into perfect fellow-
> ship with Him, filled and directed by the
> Holy Spirit and in full harmony with the
> divine essence common to the Father, Son

and Holy Spirit. It will be the humanity
of God. But it will still be humanity and
not deity - human and not divine essence.[48]

What takes place then is this: He participates in
human essence and wholly determines it making it
"an essence which exists in and with God and is
adopted and controlled and sanctified and ruled
by Him."[49] Humanity is completely ruled by the
grace of God and as such is exalted to its freedom,
"to the obedience in whose exercise it is not
superhuman but true human freedom."[50] Human
essence is further made the participant in the
presence and effective working of the Holy Spirit;
for the Son of God, who with the Father is the
source of the Spirit and also lives in the unity
of the Spirit, is also the Son of Man. In other
words, in this confrontation of the human essence
with the divine essence, human essence is permitted or allowed to serve the divine; it is given
the power to execute its act and it acts effec-
tively to participate in the mediatorial act of
the Son, being the bearer and the server of the
divine power and authority. Finally, since human
essence is so addressed by the divine, it "is
given glory and exalted to a dignity and clothed
with a majesty which the Son who assumed it and
existed in it has in common with the Father and
Holy Ghost -- the glory and dignity and majesty
of the divine nature."[51] Thus God is God in His
connection with the human essence of Jesus Christ
as it has taken place in Him and as it is indissolu-
ble in His existence. It is only in this divinely
established connection with human essence that
we can truly know God, and magnify Him, and love
Him and call upon His name.[52]

In this act of exaltation, just as in the
dynamic condescension, self-humbling of the Son of
God, we see an act of God's freedom and divine mercy.
Man is no longer far from Him, but near to Him,
"a man who even as such and precisely as such is a
man as we are, the first-born of a new humanity; the
second Adam who is still our elder brother and in

-157-

whose exaltation our own has already taken place."[53]

The question that arises is this: what really took place in this exaltation of the Son of Man to fellowship with God? Was this just the isolated history of this one man and is it to be viewed as such? It is difficult to say that the reconciliation of man with God happened in His history, i.e., the history of this one man and not the history of any other. But the unique factor in this statement and, therefore, the one upon which we lay, and rightly so, great emphasis is the fact that the singularity of this one man's history encompasses the life of every man. Jesus is true and royal man. Barth puts it this way:

> But for all its singularity, as His history, it was not and is not a private history, but a representative and therefore a public (one). His history in the place of all other men and in accomplishment of their atonement; the history of their Head, in which they all participate. Therefore, in the most concrete sense of the term, the history of this One is world history. When God was in Christ He reconciled the world to Himself (2 Cor. 5:19), and therefore us, each one of us. In this one humanity itself, our human essence, was and is elevated and exalted.[54]

The reality of our exaltation is not dependent on our acceptance of it, nor does it depend on its repetition in our lives. Before we were in any position to accept it or reject it, we were taken up into the fellowship with God for which we were ordained. The case for all men is, then, advocated and conducted by this One, all participate in Him, all are exalted with Him to true humanity. There is reality only in Him, "but there can be no question of our not being in His representative existence, as if our own obedience were not anticipated and virtually accomplished in His."[55]

It is evident, then, that there is an ontological relationship between Jesus Christ and every
man. Jesus Christ is the Lord of every man -
all Christians and non-Christians belong to Him
and can be claimed as His de iure. This ontological
relationship or connection between Jesus Christ and
all men is the legal basis of the kerygma and this
is the reason the community must have a missionary
character, i.e., because it knows that its legal
basis of faith stands also for all other men. In
this way and for this reason the kerygma does not
deal with possibilities but declares actualities.56
There is no Jesus Christ who is what He is exclusive-
ly for Himself and there is no man who is not together with the man Jesus, who is not elevated with
Him as a true covenant partner of God.

In summation we may say that the history of
Jesus Christ as the humiliated Son of God and as the
exalted Son of Man also includes our history. The
man of sin, which we all, undoubtedly, are, is
put to death in Him (this is an ontological change
in our situation and thus to live as a man of sin
is no longer a possibility for us) and the new man,
the man exalted to fellowship with God is alive
(this also being an ontological fact in which we
participate) being the only direction open for us.
This is now our being, our situation, the atmos-
phere in which we live -- no man has his being in
and of himself but is only himself as he is in
Jesus Christ. Even those who refuse to acknowledge
the reign of Christ find themselves in the domain
of His Kingdom:

> Those who in themselves are disobedient
> are claimed and absorbed by the act of
> His obedience. The Kingdom which has come
> to them in all its strangeness is the reality
> which is so transcendent and efficacious to
> them that it cannot remain a merely external
> fact hanging over them. They themselves have
> to be within it. It is necessarily made
> their own.57

In the words of the Elder Blumhardt: "Jesus is
Victor!" God has spoken His everlasting Yea to man

and to all the creation and Karl Barth seems to be sounding this triumphant chord. Again we ask, "Is he an advocate of apokatastasis?" Joseph Bettis in an article in the Scottish Journal of Theology, "Is Karl Barth a Universalist?", maintains that Barth though holding to a universal election and a universal atonement should not be so categorized since he stops short of affirming a universal salvation and allows for the "impossibility" of self-damnation.[58] Emil Brunner, on the other hand, is convinced that Barth is a universalist, one of the most thorough-going in his insistence that all mankind has already been saved through the cross and resurrection of Jesus Christ. Barth does speak in this way, but as he so often does, he also can say: "Nowhere does the New Testament say that the world is saved, nor can we say that it is without doing violence to the New Testament."[59] And at the conclusion of a later volume, "He [man] stands under the threat and danger of being damned. His condemnation hangs over him like a sword."[60]

It cannot be denied, however, that Barth's theology at least leads him in the direction of a universalism, for even the condemnation of which he speaks, to which we have just referred, is not yet a reality; but the decisive act of God in Christ is a reality, a certain reality! It is a gracious conviction that "all men and all creation are ordained to be the theatre of His glory and therefore the recipients and bearers of His Word."[61] As we have already suggested -- why not the possibility of apokatastasis -- if God be God? At the very least it must be a hope!

Enough of Barth's position, i.e., the manner in which he sees the Christological natures in the states of humiliation and exaltation, especially with respect to the doctrine of reconciliation has been presented to give us a basic understanding and foundation in his thought in this particular area. Therefore, in the succeeding chapter we shall attempt to raise a few questions concerning Karl Barth's thought, issues that are somewhat problematic in our judgment.

CHAPTER 7 NOTES

1. Karl Barth, Church Dogmatics, Volume IV/1, "The
Doctrine of Reconciliation," translated by G. W.
Bromiley (Edinburgh: T & T Clark, 1956), pp. 126-127.

2. Ibid., pp. 158ff., Cf., G. C. Berkouwer, The
Triumph of Grace in the Theology of Karl Barth (Grand
Rapids: Wm. B. Eerdmans Publishing Co., 1956), pp. 132ff.,
Cf. George S. Hendry, The Gospel of the Incarnation
(Philadelphia: The Westminster Press, 1958), p. 99.

3. Barth, Church Dogmatics, Volume IV/1, p. 147.

4. Ibid., p. 126.

5. Hendry, op. cit., pp. 98-99.

6. This was the central thought in the chapter in
which we treated Barth's doctrine of the Trinity,
most especially "The Doctrine of the Trinity as the
Immediate Implicate of Revelation."

7. Barth, Church Dogmatics, Volume IV/1, p. 164.

8. Ibid., p. 177.

9. Ibid., p. 183.

10. Ibid., p. 186.

11. Ibid.

12. Ibid., p. 187.

13. Ibid., p. 192.

14. Ibid., p. 198.

15. Ibid.

16. Ibid., p. 199. It is at this point that Barth
sharply criticizes the modalist and subordinationist
views for failing to see that the humiliation, the
lowliness, and the obedience of the one true God is
of His own essence. This ontological-economic relationship is primary for Barth.

17. Ibid., p. 164.

18. Berthold Klappert, Die Auferweckung des Gekreuzigten, Der Ansatz der Christologie Karl Barths
im Zusammenhang der Christologie der Gegenwart
(Neukrichen, 1971), p. 154.

19. Barth, Church Dogmatics, Volume IV/1, p. 215.

20. Ibid., pp. 200-201; Berkouwer, op. cit.,
pp. 130-132.

21. Berkouwer, op. cit., p. 131.

22. Ibid.

23. Barth, Church Dogmatics, Volume IV/1, pp. 202-
203. Note again a previous criticism: Barth's use
of the Trinity seems to give an ontological priority
to the third mode of being, i.e., the Spirit seems
to be ousia as well as hypostasis.

24. Ibid.

25. Ibid., p. 204.

26. In Church Dogmatics, Volume II/1, pp. 357-358,
Barth speaks of grace as the very essence of God,
but that it exists in Him in a incomprehensible
way. But if it were not real in the life of God,
it would not be a divine reality.

27. Barth, Church Dogmatics, Volume IV/1, p. 304.

28. Ibid., p. 212.

29. Ibid., p. 215.

30. Ibid., p. 216.

31. Ibid., p. 217.

32. Ibid., p. 222.

33. Ibid.

34. Ibid., p. 223.

35. Ibid.

36. Ibid.

37. Ibid., p. 125. Barth admits the usefulness, for teaching purposes, of a division between the doctrine of the person and the work of Christ on the ground that it is purely analysis. But since the question of Who Christ is cannot be answered in abstraction from the question what He does, the two, in reality cannot be separated.

38. Ibid., p. 228. Here we may see clearly that Barth formulates, in a novel way, a juridico-ontological view of the atonement.

39. Karl Barth, Church Dogmatics, Volume IV/2, "The Doctrine of Reconciliation," translated by G. W. Bromiley (Edinburgh: T & T Clark, 1958), p. 6.

40. Ibid., p. 38.

41. Ibid., p. 29.

42. Ibid., p. 38.

43. Ibid., p. 48.

44. Ibid., p. 49.

45. Ibid., p. 50. One cannot, however, but be reminded of the doctrines of the so-called "impersonal" humanity of Christ in the early Church Fathers, e.g., Cyril of Alexandria. It was problematic then and it remains a problem here. Barth is aware of, and treats of, the problem rather extensively in an excursus on the concepts of anhypostasis and enhypostasis describing, and subsequently responding to, the traditional objections to the concepts, e.g., that it is blatant docetism, or that it is superfluous. Barth argues that these will always exist and as such represent our own unbelief. However, he argues, the concepts of anhypostasis and enhypostasis are quite unavoidable if we are to correctly understand the mystery.

46. Ibid., p. 51. We made the same point earlier when we discussed Barth's interpretation of John 1:14 (see pp. 119 ff.).

47. Ibid., p. 92.

48. Ibid., p. 72.

49. Ibid., p. 88.

50. Ibid., p. 92.

51. Ibid., p. 100.

52. Ibid., pp. 100-101.

53. Ibid., p. 103.

54. Ibid., p. 269.

55. Ibid., p. 270. Was Karl Barth a universalist? Did he advocate a doctrine of apokatastasis? The entire sweep, if we may, of Barth's theology can be summed up as follows: the reconciliation of the world with God is accomplished in the life and death of Jesus Christ as atonement, revealed in the power of the resurrection, and is by the Holy Spirit, present with men through the church leading to man's final redemption. While we may accuse Barth of apokatastasis - universalism, and even though he sounds, as Bultmann suggests,a triumphant theology of grace, it is difficult to explicitly draw the conclusion that he is. Nevertheless, since his emphasis is so much on God's YES to men -- and properly so -- one must view the possibility of universalism, i.e., universal salvation or universal atonement or restoration with genuine expectation and hope. And, why not? Does not the love of God, the grace of God impel us in this direction even if we cannot say that it will definitely be so? Again, we are reminded, how often Barth alludes to our "unbelief" in God's greatness and God's grace -- not only in the Church Dogmatics -- but, indeed, in all of his writings.

56. Ibid., p. 275.

57. Karl Barth, Church Dogmatics, Volume II/2 "The Doctrine of God" (Edinburgh: T & T Clark, 1957), p. 27.

58. Joseph Bettis, "Is Karl Barth a Universalist?" The Scottish Journal of Theology, December 1967, pp. 423-436.

59. Barth, Church Dogmatics, Volume II/2, p. 423.

60. Karl Barth, Church Dogmatics, Volume IV/3, first-half, "The Doctrine of Reconciliation" (Edinburgh: T & T Clark, 1961), p. 465.

61. Ibid., p. 117.

CHAPTER VIII

CRITIQUE

As we now focus our attention on a critique of
some of the theological formulations of Karl Barth,
It is necessary to state at the outset that one
cannot help but be greatly impressed with the pro-
fundity of his thought, and yet, also with the
basically simple structure in which his thought is
framed. The architectonic proportions of his work
are indeed unmistakable. The theme of the first
great movement --- God's humbling of Himself to take
the place of man --- leads almost irresistibly
to the second movement --- man's exaltation to
fellowship with God. As a Swiss commentator once
described this great Protestant theologian's work,
it is "a massive work, which flows along like a
great river, calmly, between uninhabited shores
through an apocalyptic landscape."[1] Whatever is
said, therefore, by way of a critique, must be seen
in the light of his tremendous contribution to the
history of Christian thought.

A. THE TRINITARIAN CONCEPTION OF REVELATION AND KARL
BARTH'S ANTHROPOLOGICAL PRESUPPOSITIONS

    It is beneficial for us to begin our critical
evaluation of Barth's trinitarian conception of
revelation with a consideration of his anthropological presuppositions, for the implications of his
thinking in this area are closely connected with his
thought on reconciliation which we shall consider
next.

    In its simplest form, the self-evident frame
of reference for the whole of Barth's theology
is basically that God has a certain nature, that man
has a certain nature and that the latter has no
knowledge of the former unless the former reveals
Himself to the latter. This God has done in
Jesus Christ, i.e., "the Word became flesh" (John 1:14).
Thus revelation, the incarnation and the Trinity,
which are closely interwoven and interdependent,
become central and may be understood as a revelation of God to man, as the antithesis to natural
knowledge of God, i.e., the antithesis to the
thesis that man, of himself, by nature, does not
know anything about God. The frame of reference,
then, consists of three elements: (1) God as an

unknown being (Deus Absconditus) until He reveals Himself (Deus Revelatus), and henceforth as known; (2) man without knowledge of God and directed to the place where God reveals Himself; and finally, (3) the concept of revelation, i.e., in Jesus Christ. These are all biblical elements and the entire framework seems scriptural.

Yet as we examine Barth's thought we see that there is a definite shift of emphasis from the death and resurrection of Jesus Christ to the incarnation, from the Cross of Calvary to the manger of Bethlehem, a shift of emphasis which is primarily based upon Barth's fundamental anthropological presupposition, i.e., that man lacks a certain knowledge of God. This change naturally corresponds to the shifting of the center in regard to the content of scripture. That is to say, it is possible to retain the death and resurrection at the center only if, anthropologically, we think in terms of conflict and of guilt, and therefore reckon with something actively evil in man, an evil that must die or be destroyed in order that a new man may arise. When the human predicament is conceived in these terms, a change becomes necessary in the human condition of man, and the struggle of the death and resurrection of Christ must remain central. But Barth does not see the problem in these terms; rather he sees the problem in terms of the human situation, i.e., in man's lack of knowledge, something which man does not possess. When viewed in this way sin becomes an "unreality," and an "impossibility," "das Nichtige," which can only exist on the basis of an ontological misunderstanding or mistake (or perhaps on man's mistaken notion of defiance?). When the death and resurrection of Jesus Christ yield their place in the center of the kerygma to the incarnation, this corresponding anthropological change also occurs. God's appearance in human form becomes central and the primary function of faith is to apprehend this appearance in human form by God. Faith then apprehends God and acquires knowledge of Him - a knowledge which man did not previously possess.[2] There is no question of a conflict between good and evil; it is non-essential. "The essential element is a chasm, an interval, a real distance between God and man and across the chasm, a reflection, a reproduction of the higher in the dark surface of the lower."

Everything is cast into this Platonic frame of
reference which is never broken.[3]

While we may appreciate the great service which
Karl Barth has rendered to trinitarian theology
by the emphasis and prominence he gives to it
in his own theology, we may also see that the
way in which he has used and applied it has been
considerably expensive. This is evident in the
application of his trinitarian conception of
revelation in the sphere of anthropology. Several
criticisms may be made:

First: Although Barth does speak of the death
and resurrection of Jesus Christ, it is clear that
the revelation, i.e., the incarnation, is the real
point of significance for him. In his preoccupation
with this aspect of the faith, Barth, like the
early Greek Fathers, with whom he is very sympathe-
tic, is fragmenting the gospel. Furthermore, it
is this preoccupation with the incarnation that
enables Barth to see the whole problem in terms of
two parties, God and man, without the existence
of an evil force or power. But is this the biblical conception? Is he really true to the biblical
witness? Is his analysis correct?

Second: There is much emphasis placed on man's
lack of the knowledge of God. The decisive factor
being that the man into whose world God enters
is a man without the knowledge of God, a man without
contact with God. But is this the kind of man
described in the scriptures? And what are we to
say of God's revelation to Israel? Is man really
completely without the knowledge of God as Barth
maintains?[4]

Third: The subjective element in this experience between God and man, i.e., in God's self-
unveiling, is at the very most a noetic experience,
an experience which is definitely subordinate to
the objective event of God's revelation (which,
of course, we see analyzed in the doctrine of the
Trinity). For Barth holds that man has not the
capacity to respond to this act but must first
receive all capacity. And he writes, further, that
the experience of the Word of God always takes
place in an act of human self-determination, but
it is not as this act that it is experience of the

-171-

Word of God. The fact of knowledge of the Word of
God does not presuppose its possibility in man,
but in coming to man it brings the possibility with
it. Therefore, in the last analysis, man's role
in the God, man, revelation structure is basically
unimportant, and the response that he makes, from
his point of view, is really a shallow and empty
response.

B. THE TRINITARIAN CONCEPTION OF REVELATION AND
RECONCILIATION

     We may see a second application of Karl Barth's
notion in his doctrine of reconciliation. This
second consideration is very much like the preceding
one for here also Barth sees the problem of the
atonement and reconciliation not in terms of the human
condition of sinful man but in terms of the human
situation which needs to be rectified. We must say,
however, that Barth's understanding of the gravity
of the human situation is the greatest merit or
contribution of his doctrine, i.e, the fact that
the necessity of the atonement arises not from the
inexorable requirements of divine justice which
must be satisfied before God can exercise His mercy,
but rather from the objective realities in this
human situation which have been caused by sin.[5] It
is this human sin, the so-called "ontological impossibility or absurdity," that is the disturbing
factor in creation and it is this very same human
sin that is the obstacle which disrupts the covenant
relation between God and man. Reconciliation,
therefore, is, as understood and analyzed by
Barth, a change in this human situation, i.e.,
the removal of sin, the restoration of creation
out of chaos. God accomplishes this task, i.e.,
reconciles man to Himself, by taking upon Himself
human creatureliness, and therefore, by placing
Himself in the position of alienation. In this
event we have a manifestation of the unveiling
of the veiled, the Word becoming flesh, i.e., the
solution articulated in terms of the trinitarian
conception of revelation, Barth's central thrust.

     Furthermore, considered in terms of this
trinitarian concept of revelation, this act, this
event, is not just a mere possibility, but it is a
reality, an accomplished act, a completed event.

That is to say, redemption and pardon took place in Him, in Jesus Christ, illic et tunc and in significance hic et nunc. This event of reconciliation, which takes place in the history of the unity of God and man, oriented in the framework of revelation, cannot be dissolved or diluted or destroyed; but rather it must be considered as the reality that it is. Thus we see a real stress on the objective nature of reconciliation as a real transformation of the human situation, which is perfectly in line with the way in which we described Barth's anthropological presupposition and its implications.

As in the case of our brief consideration of the anthropological situation, if Barth's thought is completely acceptable then we can say, quite simply, that the problem of the reconciliation of man have been solved. For example, in the problem of the objective and the subjective: these two elements have been related in such a way that the objective event --- Jesus Christ --- (revelation) includes in Himself the subjective response needed in order that reconciliation may be accomplished, i.e., a subjective response which includes the response of every man. But Barth sees this relationship, in which the subjective is included in the objective, integrated in such a way that one does not absorb the other. If we can accept this position our problems are apparently solved.

However, we cannot and the fundamental structure of the trinitarian conception of revelation also causes certain difficulties when applied to reconciliation. It may be seen quite clearly in this subject-object relation, for while Barth attempts to give some place to the subjective side of reconciliation by including it as a part of the objective content of this event, in actuality, the subjective is absorbed in the objective, making it at the most a noetic experience, an experience which is definitely subordinate to the objective event and which is in the last analysis really quite unimportant in that it does not in the least change the reality of man's relationship to and with God. In other words, we may ask, does not Barth's treatment of the subjective run the risk of presenting the reconciliation as a divine drama, played out over and above the life of man as a tour de force, accomplished by God for man which is man's heritage whatever man does on the plane of his historical existence? Man is placed in this situation, i.e., in the embrace of divine grace, from the very beginning of his existence, and from all eternity, so that he never really seems to reach a position from which he assumes a free relation to God. Barth does seek to accord a real freedom to man, e.g., man is free to say NO to God, but since God has said already, from all eternity, NO to negation, man's NO is overruled by God's YES. Is it not true, therefore, that Barth's objectivity, which we see as a natural consequence of the application of his trinitarian conception of revelation to all areas of the Christian faith, is so severe that even the experience of the Christian individual can only be interpreted as referring to their knowledge of their participation in the objective event of reconciliation, as the description of the movement of the life of Jesus Christ which they know as the reality that encompasses their lives? He therefore reduces reconciliation, because his anthropological presuppositions and his concept of revelation make it necessary, from the point of view of man, to a purely noetic or cognitive apprehension of what has already taken place. In adopting this stance Barth has closed all doors to tension and division, between possibility and actuality, between the work of Christ for us, and our response to this work, by including the latter in the former, by making subjectivity an integral part of the one perfect work of Jesus Christ.

It is apparent in our brief examination of Barth's understanding of reconciliation within the framework of his trinitarian concept of revelation that the austere objective emphasis of this frame of reference causes substantial difficulty and raises serious questions in the thought of Karl Barth.

C. GENERAL OBSERVATIONS AND COMMENTS

Since we have already pointed to the significance of Karl Barth's conception of the doctrine of the Trinity, in bringing our work to a conclusion, we shall recall some of the questions

raised during the course of our discussions and
investigations with specific respect to this doctrine.

First: While we may agree with Barth that it
is necessary to base the doctrine of the Trinity
on the single root of revelation and that we
should not root the doctrine in any illustration,
this should not, however, preclude the possibility
of attempting to illustrate the concept of the
Trinity providing that we recognize and understand
the relative appropriateness and usefulness of the
illustration. It is really quite difficult to
perceive any qualitative distinction between Barth's
conception of illustration, which he rejects, and
interpretation, which he sustains.

Second: The position which Barth maintains in
his doctrines of internal relations is not always
consistent. For example, in our section on the
"Divine Unity and Variety," we noted that in one
place Barth asserts that if we are to take revelation seriously, as the presence of God, then in no
sense can we say that Jesus Christ and the Spirit
are subordinate hypostases, i.e., the Producer
must always be equal to His Product which is
Himself in distinction. Then, just a few pages
later, while discussing the very same point, Barth
asserts that the divine modes are inequal in their
original relations.[6] Is it possible to uphold
this seeming contradiction? Can God be inequal to
Himself, even in distinction? If it is God Who
subsists in His three modes of existence and not
the modes themselves that actually subsist in Him,
as Barth maintains, then this inequality is untenable.

Third: We noted that in Karl Barth contemporary theology finds a powerful defender of the concept of the double procession. However, several
questions may be raised concerning his treatment of
this subject. Even assuming that Barth's presuppositions and analyses are correct (and this is
a generous assumption), does he not attribute more
to the third mode of existence, i.e., the Holy
Spirit, in that this mode is the unifying bond within
the Godhead, than he does to the other two hypostases?
Would it not then be more natural to identify the
Spirit with ousia of God rather than with the

-175-

hypostases? Or is this hypostatic unification by the Spirit even possible? Furthermore, if this is the correct interpretation does this not imply an ontological priority of the Spirit over the Father and the Son entailing a relative subordinationism of the Father? And finally, is there any real need, except for Karl Barth's insistence on the exact conformity of the immanent Trinity with the economic Trinity, for a binding together of the Godhead? Is it necessary for them to be bound by the Spirit into that in which they already exist? Barth himself is quite explicit that the three modes of existence participate in each other, "inexist" in each other and in the divine ousia. Therefore, his position seems to be merely arbitrary being necessitated by a previous commitment to conformity in every detail.

We stated in our introduction to our discussion of the Trinity that the basic problem of the Trinity was closely related to the problem of the incarnation. In our analysis of Karl Barth's position we have seen how he comes to grips with this problem by analyzing what takes place in the event of revelation, which he sees as its root, by reaching back from the Trinity of manifestation to the ontological Trinity and by invoking the aid of such principles as the doctrine of appropriations and the concept of circumincession, co-inherence or perichoresis. Furthermore, we have also seen what takes place when Barth employs the doctrine of the Trinity as the immediate implication of revelation as a frame of reference for the Christian faith, e.g., in anthropology and reconciliation. The strong emphasis upon the objective event of revelation, which is analyzed by the doctrine of the Trinity, seems to place limitations upon the dogmatic usefulness of this doctrine.

It is our opinion, therefore, that as an interpretation of revelation, as an intellectual formulation of the concept of the Trinity, Barth's doctrine is engaging, challenging and useful, i.e., useful as a defensive instrument for the Tri-unity of God. However, as a dogmatic tool, we have seen that its usefulness and biblical accuracy are quite questionable. Nevertheless, while we may disagree with him at points, or remain unconvinced by his treatment and argumentation, we may at least be instructed by his profound thought, intellectual integrity and personal courage. As the late Professor John Baillie, who so often disagreed with Barth, once put it:

> Whatever the measure of our agreement or
> disagreements with him we have all to reckon
> with him. I have often said that there can
> be no hopeful forward advance beyond his
> teaching, as I fervently hope there will
> be, if we attempt to go round it instead
> of through it.[7]

CHAPTER 8 NOTES

1. Quoted from an article by George S. Hendry, "The
Dogmatic Form of Barth's Theology," in Theology
Today, Volume XIII, No. 3, p. 310.

2. We say this quite clearly in the section dealing
with the "Knowability of the Word of God" (pp. 55ff.)
and in the section on the "Root of the Doctrine
of the Trinity" particularly the analysis of the
statement "God reveals Himself" (pp. 76ff.). We
should remind ourselves that this is an acknowledgment, a cognition that man cannot consummate or
confirm, but is received from outside himself,
i.e., from God.

3. Gustav Wingren, Theology in Conflict (Philadelphia:
Muhlenberg Press, 1958), p. 119.

4. Earlier we argued that the doctrine of the Trinity
grounded in revelation does not exclude a revelation that is other than the trinitarian conception,
but that the trinitarian conception enrichs the
monotheism of an analogia entis.

5. Karl Barth, Church Dogmatics, Volume I/1, "The
Doctrine of the Word of God" (Edinburgh: T & T
Clark, 1960), p. 224.

6. Ibid., pp. 404-406; pp. 414-416.

7. John Baillie, The Sense of the Presence of God
(Edinburgh: T & T Clark, 1962), p. 255.

SELECTED BIBLIOGRAPHY

Anselm, St., "Monologium," in St. Anselm, translated
    by S. N. Deane, Chicago, 1962.

Augustine, St., Confessions and Enchiridion, Library
    of Christian Classics, Volume VII, translated
    by Albert C. Outler, Philadelphia, 1955.

Augustine, St., On the Trinity, Library of Christian
    Classics, Volume VIII, Philadelphia, 1955.

Baillie, Donald M., God Was In Christ, New York,
    1948.

Baillie, John, The Sense of the Presence of God,
    Edinburgh, 1962.

Balthasar, Hans Ur von., The Theology of Karl Barth,
    New York, 1971.

Barth, Karl, Action in Waiting, Rifton, New York,
    1969.

_____, Against the Stream, New York, 1954.

_____, Anselm: Fides Quarens Intellectum,
    Richmond, 1960.

_____, Christ and Adam, London, 1956.

_____, Epistle to the Philippians, Richmond,
    1962.

_____, Here and Now, New York, 1964.

_____, The Heidelberg Catechism for Today,
    Richmond, 1964.

_____, The Knowledge of God and The Service
    of God, London, 1949.

_____, Table-Talk, recorded and edited by
    John Godsay. Richmond, 1963.

_____, The Faith of the Church: A Commentary
    on the Apostles' Creed according to John
    Calvin's Catechism, New York, 1958.

_____, "No," Natural Theology and Grace and the reply "No" by Dr. Karl Barth, London, 1946.

_____, Protestant Theology in the 19th Century, Valley Forge, Pa., 1972.

_____, The Resurrection of the Dead, New York, 1933.

_____, Die Christliche Dogmatik im Entworf: Die Lehre vom Worte Gottes: Prolegomena zur Christlichen Dogmatik, Munich, 1927.

_____, "On Systematic Theology," The Scottish Journal of Theology, Volume 14, No. 3, September, 1961.

_____, Dogmatics in Outline, New York, 1947.

_____, "Revelation," in Revelation, edited by John Baillie and Hugh Martin, London, 1937.

_____, God, Gospel, and Grace, Edinburgh, 1959.

_____, Credo, New York, 1962.

_____, The Word of God and The Word of Man, New York, 1957.

_____, The Humanity of God, Richmond, 1960.

_____, The Epistle to the Romans, Oxford, 1935.

_____, Theology and Church, London, 1962.

_____, Evangelical Theology: An Introduction, New York, 1963.

_____, Church Dogmatics: The Doctrine of the Word of God, Volume I/1, Edinburgh, 1960.

_____, Church Dogmatics: The Doctrine of the Word of God, Volume I/2, Edinburgh, 1956.

_____, Church Dogmatics: The Doctrine of God, Volume II/1, Edinburgh, 1957.

_____, Church Dogmatics: The Doctrine of God, Volume II/2, Edinburgh, 1957.

_____, Church Dogmatics: The Doctrine of Creation, Volume III/1, Edinburgh, 1958.

_____, Church Dogmatics: The Doctrine of Creation, Volume III/2, Edinburgh, 1960.

_____, Church Dogmatics: The Doctrine of Reconciliation, Volume IV/1, Edinburgh, 1956.

_____, Church Dogmatics: The Doctrine of Reconciliation, Volume IV/2, Edinburgh, 1958.

_____, Church Dogmatics: The Doctrine of Reconciliation, Volume IV/3, First-Half, Edinburgh, 1961.

_____, Church Dogmatics: The Doctrine of Reconciliation, Volume IV/3, Second-Half, Edinburgh, 1962.

Berkouwer, G. C., The Triumph of Grace in the Theology of Karl Barth, Grand Rapids, 1956.

Bloesch, Donald, Jesus is Victor! Nashville, 1976.

Brunner, Emil, The Christian Doctrine of God, Philadelphia, 1950.

Bettis, Joseph, "Is Barth a Universalist?" in The Scottish Journal of Theology, December, 1967.

Calvin, John, Institutes of the Christian Religion, Grand Rapids, 1957.

Come, Arnold, An Introduction to Barth's Dogmatics for Preachers, Philadelphia, 1963.

Feuerbach, Ludwig, The Essence of Christianity, New York, 1957.

Franks, Robert S., The Doctrine of the Trinity, London, 1953.

Godsey, John, How I Changed My Mind? Richmond, 1966.

Gregory of Nyssa, "On 'Not Being Three Gods'" trans-
lated by Cyril Richardson in Christology of the
Later Fathers, Library of Christian Classics,
Volume III, Philadelphia, 1954.

Gregory of Nazianzen, "The Theological Orations,"
translated by C. B. Brown and J. E. Swallow
in Christology of the Later Fathers, Library
of Christian Classics, Volume III, Philadelphia,
1954.

Hausmann, William John, Karl Barth's Doctrine of
Election, New York, 1969.

Hendry, George S., "The Dogmatics Form of Barth's
Theology," Theology Today, Volume XIII, No. 3,
October, 1956.

_____, "Barth for Beginners," Theology Today,
Volume XIX, July, 1962.

_____, The Gospel of the Incarnation, Phila-
delphia, 1958.

_____, The Holy Spirit in Christian Theology,
Philadelphia, 1956.

Hodgson, Leonard, The Doctrine of the Trinity, New
York, 1944.

Irenaeus of Lyons, Against Heresies in the Ante-
Nicene Fathers, Grand Rapids, 1956.

Klappert, Berthold, Die Auferweckung des Gekreuzigten,
Der Ansatz der Christologie Karl Barths im
Zusammenhang der Christologie der Gegenwort,
Neukrichen, 1971.

Knight, J. A. T., "A Biblical Approach to the Doctrine
of the Trinity," The Scottish Journal of Theology,
Occasional Papers, Edinburgh, 1958.

Kung, Hans, Justification, New York, 1964.

Matczak, Sebastian, _Karl Barth on God_, New York, 1962.

Prestige, G. L., _God in Patristic Thought_, London, 1936.

Rawlinson, A. E. J., _Essays on the Trinity and the Incarnation_, London, 1928.

Richardson, Cyril D., _The Doctrine of the Trinity_, New York, 1958.

Smart, James, Editor, _Revolutionary Theology in the Making: Barth-Thurneysen Correspondence 1914-1925_, Richmond, 1964.

Thompson, John, _Christ in Perspective: Christological Perspectives in the Theology of Karl Barth_, Grand Rapdis, 1978.

Tillich, Paul, "The Present Theological Situation in the Light of the Continental European Development," _Theology Today, Volume VI_, October, 1949.

_____, _Systematic Theology in Three Volumes_, New York, 1965.

Torrance, Thomas F., _Karl Barth: An Introduction to His Early Thought_, 1910-1931, Edinburgh, 1958.

Wainwright, Arthur, _The Trinity in the New Testament_, London, 1962.

Wingren, Gustaf., _Theology in Conflict_, Philadelphia, 1958.